Lite,
Leadership
and the
Pursuit of Happiness

Order this book online at www.trafford.com
or email orders@trafford.com

Most Trafford titles are also available at major online book retailers.

Printed in Victoria, BC, Canada.

ISBN: 978-1-4269-0730-2 (sc)
ISBN: 978-1-4269-0731-9 (hc)
ISBN: 978-1-4269-0732-6 (eb)

*Our mission is to efficiently provide the world's finest, most comprehensive
book publishing service, enabling every author to experience success.
To find out how to publish your book, your way, and have it available
worldwide, visit us online at www.trafford.com*

Trafford rev. 1/25/10

 www.trafford.com

North America & international
toll-free: 1 888 232 4444 (USA & Canada)
phone: 250 383 6864 ♦ fax: 812 355 4082

Life, Leadership and the Pursuit of Happiness

Encouragements for Living a Significant Life

By William F. Hart

Trafford Publishing
Bloomington, Indiana · USA

This book is dedicated to my two daughters,
Varina and Chaffin

"There is no status quo in living your life. If you are not moving forward in life, then you are moving backward."

Acknowledgments

Thanks to my parents, Joe and Pet Hart, for teaching me Biblical truths, for giving me a great education and for always being there.

Thanks to my wife, Varina, who has encouraged me on this project, and to friends and family who helped me make this book a reality. Thanks for my pastor for preaching Biblical truths. Thanks to Zig Ziglar for encouraging me to become a life leader at a seminar in 1986.

Thanks to my parents and to Gini and Julie for editing.

Contents

Introduction

Life, Leadership and the Pursuit of Happiness!

In the daily living of life, I wanted to pass on to my children, family, friends and acquaintances valuable life lessons that I have learned. A passion of mine is continuous learning; for I feel if I am not moving forward, then it is backward I go. Out of this passion comes a joy for sharing with others what I have learned or am continuously learning. Thus, I conceived a newsletter. From several years' worth of newsletters, I have compiled this book.

I chose the title *LIFE, LEADERSHIP AND THE PURSUIT OF HAPPINESS* because I feel we are in a leadership crisis in our current times. Our founding fathers declared that we have certain inalienable rights of life, liberty and the pursuit of happiness. To possess true liberty, each individual must practice personal leadership as a route to Life Leadership. Personal leadership is required, because true liberty is not achieved unless a person can demonstrate continual personal leadership – i.e. Life Leadership. Without personal leadership, you become a slave to circumstances and a victim in your mind. You become trapped by your own thinking, denying yourself the true opportunity to pursue happiness. People who are victims of their minds believe that life is all about *them*. Unfortunately, this is just the opposite of achieving true happiness.

This book is about the true pursuit of happiness and achieving happiness, the way we were originally designed to achieve happiness. It is also about having true relationships – with others and with the great lover of our souls.

The time to be reflective about your life is now! This book on

2

Life Leadership is as much a reminder for me as it is a way to share these lessons with others.

    This is a weekly reading to share and to encourage you in your life journey. The two topics that I hold dearest are the walk of faith and personal leadership. To get the most out of this book, read each lesson **6 times per week**. It takes at least 6 times not only to grasp a concept, but also to truly apply the lesson. Repetition is the mother of all learning. May your first application be by learning through repetition.

Blessings to all,

Bill Hart

Life Quotes by Bill Hart

"A Life Leader does not allow circumstances of today to control his or her tomorrow."

"Life Leaders plan for the future and do not let the future plan them."

"Having purpose and working toward that purpose on a daily basis is the foundation of a Life Leader."

"Life Leaders live a balanced life. They are prepared."

"Being others-focused is a true mark of a Life Leader."

"Life Leaders have endurance in hard times, because they prepared; they don't wing life."

"Life Leaders teach their children to handle life by example and by a planned approach. They raise their children versus letting society raise them."

"Goals help you have courage to say 'no' to how other people live their life, so you can live *your* life achieving *your* goals."

The Power of Affirmations

Affirmations are mentioned throughout this book. Affirmations are personal, present-tense statements about yourself, related to how you want to become, what you want to be. You say them to yourself as though you are already there. Through affirmations you program or re-program your mind. Examples are: "I weigh 180 lbs." "I am a good listener." "I love my neighbor by speaking to him or her each day."

By using affirmations, you are retraining your mind to become what you want it to be. The key to successfully using affirmations is that they must be present tense – "I am" vs. "I will" and not "I want" or "I will try...." You must recite these out loud to yourself daily. By hearing yourself say them, you will begin to believe them. Most people already use affirmations but don't realize it. They say to themselves, "You are a loser." "I am so fat." "I can't do that." "I am no good." "I always fail." "No one loves me."

Others do use affirmations positively when they talk to themselves: "I will win." "I am a kind person." Affirmations are just talking to yourself in a planned, proactive manner versus a reactive manner. Successful people are proactive, even in their self-conscious talk. Affirmations are the way to change yourself. Zig Ziglar says it perfectly when he says "You change what you are and where you are by first changing what goes into your mind." Affirmations are the secret to successful change. This is what the Bible means when it says to "renew your mind." Ziglar says to "put the pure, powerful, the clean and the positive into your mind."

Why This Book?

The purpose of this book is to ask a fundamental question and motivate people to change. The question is, "Are you leading in life, or is life leading you?" If life is leading you, then you are going nowhere in particular. You are letting life happen, which generally delivers disappointment and broken relationships. At the latter stages of your life, many will typically say, "I wish I had done more."

Are you a "wondering generality" who lets circumstances control you, or are you leading in your life? Do you consciously work on continuous improvement in your life in the areas of faith, marriage, children, work, health, finances, social relationships and community? You get the picture. Life Leadership is telling yourself "If I am not moving forward, then I am moving backward," and then working to keep yourself moving forward. Life Leadership takes the attitude of "Do it now!" You cannot say to yourself, "I'll begin tomorrow," for tomorrow never really comes. This attitude is one of procrastination and lets circumstances or other people dictate what commands your time, energy and relationships. Life Leadership says, "I am a giver, not a taker." Life Leadership says, "I am not a victim, no matter what the circumstances."

You see Life Leaders getting involved in other people's lives. You see Life Leaders caring for their wives or husbands. You see Life Leaders making a difference. Life Leaders face difficult circumstances with a positive attitude, always looking for the best. Life Leaders trust others. Life Leaders are not sedentary; they are active. Life Leaders have faith.

People being led by life through circumstances, other people, laziness, or even the media and popular culture are like a river just going with flow. Unfortunately, the flow leads them nowhere in particular. And as we know, most water runs downriver and then into the sea to be indistinguishable from everything else.

People being led by life focus more on their personal entertainment than on relationships. They focus on personal pleasure versus good health. People being led by life almost always choose the easiest route or the task that requires the least amount of work. These people are controlled by others or are just cruising along with personal happiness for the moment as their immediate goal.

Does the sole pursuit of personal happiness really deliver personal happiness? The answer is no! Personal happiness or significance comes in the pursuit of helping others, building relationships, seeking the best in a situation, developing your faith, and trusting God. It is in these things that true happiness comes. To have true liberty to pursue happiness, a person must show those facets of Life Leadership.

Sadly, some of the easiest things to do to become a Life Leader are the easiest things to neglect. Life Leaders turn off the TV and instead read a book. Non-Life Leaders, or "followers," assume TV or entertainment is a right. Life Leaders evaluate their health, because others depend on them to be healthy. Followers don't care about their health, thinking, "It is my body, and I can do what I want." Life Leaders consider others when making decisions, while followers consider themselves most important.

Life Leaders practice self-discipline and self-control. Life Leaders are living a life of continuous improvement, not a life of continuous decline. In nature and life, there is no status quo. Either things are being made to improve or they are, by nature, declining from order to disorder.

Which way are you going? Are you being led by the nose, or are you leading? Be a Life Leader today; make the choice now!!

I read this _ _ _ _ _ _ _ times this week.

Starting the New Year

Starting a new year requires reflecting on the past year, where we succeeded and where we failed. The beginning of a new year is a blessing because, psychologically, it allows us to start over. "OK, I did not do what I should have done last year, but I can start over this year." But many people have trouble starting over, for they are caught in the grief or rut of their mistakes. Grieving over your mistakes is good if it leads to repentance and change of behavior, but grieving is a waste of time if it is full of self-pity and does not lead to change. Most grieve over their mistakes in how mistakes affected themselves, not how they affected others. When you grieve over how mistakes affect others that can lead to change.

Forward Focus

Starting over requires you to forgive yourself, learn from your mistakes and then work to not repeat them. Starting off the new year requires you to have a forward-looking focus, not the reverse. Set your goals; define the actions you need to take, the attitudes you need to promote, and the relationships you need to mend or build; then work on them. Not forgiving yourself actually leads you right back into the same behavior that caused you problems in the first place. If you are habitually repeating failures, forgive yourself, set a plan, and then take action.

If you have not planned for this year, take this week to identify 3-4 goals you want to achieve this year. (Too many will lead to feeling overwhelmed.) Make them specific, measurable, reasonable and attainable. Develop a plan of action in writing and then post these goals on your bathroom mirror or other place of significance.

The first thing to work on is your attitude, for it is your conscious and unconscious thoughts that lead you forward or get

8

you into a rut. As a person thinks, so he or she acts. As Zig Ziglar says, "You change what you are and where you are by changing what goes into your mind." Set goals to read wholesome material. I work to read 20 books a year. This may be a bit ambitious for someone starting out, so start with five. Don't just read for entertainment; read for attitude change. Use affirmations to change your attitude, which leads to behavioral change. Listen to CDs or tapes on personal development – listen to them over and over, for it is through repetition that we learn and change. Make your car your new classroom. Don't just listen to music or talk radio, listen to learn and listen to improve.

Several good authors to read or listen to their audios are: Jim Rohn, Zig Ziglar, Philip Yancey, Billy Graham, Napoleon Hill, Billy Cox and the best seller... The Bible.

Happy New Year!

Faith

Micah 7: 18-19 – *"Who is a God like you who pardons sin and forgives the transgression of the remnant of his inheritance? You do not stay angry forever but delight to show mercy. You will again have compassion on us: you will tread our sins underfoot and hurl all our iniquities into the depths of the sea."*

One of the hardest things to do is to forgive yourself. When I screw up and see how badly I screwed up and the horrible consequences, I feel horrible. I ask, "How could I have been so foolish or stupid?" I beat myself over the head with my mistake, and it can take a long time to forgive myself, if ever.

Two things are reflected in this situation:

1) I assume that I am wonderful and am not prone to make great mistakes. That is called pride.

2) My pride won't let me forgive myself.

I see in Micah that God pardons my sins and totally forgives my transgressions. He is not angry with me but delights in showing mercy and forgiveness. If God can forgive me, then who am I that I cannot forgive myself?

I am to rest in God's forgiveness and live in thankfulness and work to serve Him.

I read this _ _ _ _ _ _ times this week.

Deciding to Change

In life we face challenges: relationships, work, physical, emotional, financial, spiritual and educational, just to name a few. Many times we have goals or desires in these areas that seem out of reach. In reality, under your current circumstances they may indeed be out of reach. To achieve your goals requires change. Stopping pain, building a relationship, getting a degree or achieving a new level requires you to do something out of the ordinary. How "out of the ordinary" your goals are or the life changes you need will determine how willing you are to work to achieve the goal.

Dealing with Today's Circumstances

In today's world, a person will have to change to survive. What we once relied upon may no longer exist, such as Social Security, a close community, "traditional" ways of doing things or family members. Those who are willing to embrace change will survive; those who won't embrace change will eventually embrace pain, hardship and emotional distress.

If you are not working to be your best from the inside out, then you are letting the outside in, becoming what the environment around you will force you to become. Unfortunately, that is generally a mixed-up mess. Society sends too many mixed messages for a person to truly become whole, goal-directed and self-sufficient. Society applauds a good character trait one moment and an immoral character trait the next. You must consciously work to become the person who you want to be, from the inside out.

Are You Stuck?

Many people are miserably stuck in a particular situation because change appears to be a greater risk or fear than the present situation. They are on one side of the river and can see the blessing on the other, but they are afraid to cross the river.

They have learned to live within their misery instead of doing something about it.

If you are in this situation, what is keeping you from change?

1) Comfort. Change may mean getting out of your comfort zone, the area where you are competent, know all the boundaries, and where you feel secure.

2) Fear of what "might" happen if you change or don't succeed. Zig Ziglar says fear, most of the time, is really **F.E.A.R.** – **F**alse **E**vidence **A**ppearing **R**eal. You imagine or see something that "could" happen, and you believe and act upon it as if it IS going to happen.

3) Others. Unfortunately for most, blaming others or the economy (or whatever) is just a lame excuse to not hold yourself accountable.

4) Not enough money. The lack of money seems real until you see what others have done with less. Not having money is just an excuse. Too many people have overcome that obstacle.

5) Belief. You don't believe you can achieve the change. Start working on your belief through affirmations and by surrounding yourself with those who believe in you. Read books on how others overcame obstacles. "Where there is a will, there is a way."

6) Just don't want to. This is typically because a person does not have a purpose in his or her life which includes the betterment of others. Typically, this attitude is that the end result is not clearly defined in terms of benefit to yourself or to others. When people see a clearly defined goal and understand and see what the benefit to them is, they then want to move forward.

There are several good tools to help you change: affirmations, pictures, clearly defined goals with the benefit, your friends, your family and counselors. Spend time to identify what the desired outcome should be; get others to help you in this process.

Reading is the Process to Change

Amazingly, the average American reads less than 3 books per year. Most of those books have nothing to do with becoming a better person or building better people. I used to read a little but decided that I wanted to change, so I set a hearty goal of 20 books per year. I was surprised at how easy the goal was to reach when I stopped watching TV during weeknights. I posted the goal on my mirror, which motivated me to achieve it. Also, I did not require books of a certain length; any book of any length was OK. The point is that I am now reading a lot.

If you want to change, start reading and turn off the TV. Get books on tape or CD. Listen to motivational CDs or podcasts; listen to the Bible on CD or download good material. You can only change who you are when you change what you put into your mind.

Life Leaders realize change is required to live a wholesome, fulfilling life.

Faith

Romans 12: 2 – *"Do not conform any longer to the pattern of this world, but be transformed by the renewing of your minds. Then you will be able to test and approve what God's will is – his good, pleasing and perfect will."*

True change requires us to first change our attitudes. Our attitudes are changed when our mind is renewed. A regular feeding on God's word (not just church once a week) will bring about a transformation. Because the attitudes of the world are so strong, we must regularly (4+ times per week) renew our minds with God's word. I have found that to keep my mind renewed, I must renew my mind throughout the day, starting with reading scripture in the morning, having verses in my car or listening to wholesome music. This helps combat the negatives that I get from today's culture.

In my own life, my faith was strengthened and attitudes changed when I memorized scripture. I had become lazy and had not done that in several years. I have started again. I write verses on 3x5 cards and carry them in my car. I am memorizing God's promises, such as Psalms 23 or Philippians 4: 4-8. These verses keep my head and attitude in the right place as we face these difficult economic times. They remind me that God is in control no matter what happens.

Blessings to all this year.

I read this _ _ _ _ _ _ _ times this week

Opportunity

For the past 12 months, I have been trying to get a business going. I spent 6 months on one venture and the opportunity ended in the ditch. I am now working on another. Instead of being discouraged, I have realized that we live in the greatest land with the greatest opportunities. If first you don't succeed, look for another opportunity. Nowhere else in the world does this environment exist! If you don't like what you are doing, go do something else! Wow! What an incredible country we live in! Too often, we focus on what we don't have or what bad circumstances are happening without ever comparing ourselves to other countries or other times in history.

My new reply for when someone asks me, "How's it going?" is to answer, "Incredible! The streets are paved with gold!" or, "Incredible; opportunity abounds everywhere. I just have to go out and get it!" or, "With this much effort something great is gong to happen." Those replies are reminders for me of the opportunities and blessings I have. What I speak is really for me, but hopefully, others will be encouraged, too. Those are my affirmations to keep me looking ahead, not behind and for me to keep a positive attitude.

Having a positive attitude in tough times delivers a whole lot more than having a negative attitude in such times. Many people ask "What good is a positive attitude when times are tough?" I reply "What good does a negative attitude do?" For a negative attitude sees nothing but gloom and no opportunity for a better future. A positive attitude works for a better future no matter what the present circumstances are. It is your choice, do you believe in a better future, then show it with a positive attitude.

Faith

In light of my business ventures and the struggles we face, it is easy to get bogged down by the past. But solely thinking about the past does not take us anywhere but down. The Apostle Paul reminds us in Philippians 3: 13-14 – *"But one thing I do: Forgetting what is behind and straining toward what is ahead, I press on toward the goal to win the prize for which God has called me heavenward in Christ Jesus."*

Two questions:

1) Are you looking at the past, or do you have a future focus? If you are looking to the past, then you are stuck or actually moving backwards. Looking back immobilizes; looking positively into the future motivates.

2) Is your goal or life direction strictly for you, or is there a heavenly aspect to this goal or direction?

If something always gets in the way of your goal, then your goal is probably not clearly defined in terms of steps to achieve it, nor is the benefit to you and others clearly defined. In that case, it is not a goal, but just a hope or wish. Creating a goal requires hard work and focus, but it is well worth it.

May your day be blessed as you seek opportunity and share it with others. Make a smile and pass it on!

I read this _ _ _ _ _ _ _ times this week.

Wheel of Life

Our lives are multi-dimensional, not just work, play, health or relationships. All aspects are interconnected, much like a wheel with many spokes. There are eight areas of our life that need continual development: career, physical and health, spiritual and ethical, mental and educational, social and cultural, family and home, financial and, last, recreational.

Each of these areas is like a spoke on a wheel. The wheel is your life. The hub is your soul. If one or more spokes are out of true, too long or too short, or aren't even in the hub, you are leading an imbalanced life. An imbalanced life causes pain (to yourself and to others), unfulfilled dreams and incompleteness in your life. A person living a balanced life gives attention to developing or nurturing each area of his or her life on a regular basis. People leading a balanced life enjoy life and have purpose; others also enjoy the fruit of their efforts. Creating and maintaining a balanced wheel requires a conscious assessment of where you are strong and where you need development. Then the process requires an intentional plan with specifics and deadlines of what can be done.

Short-Term vs. Long-Term Neglect

There are times in our lives where one or more spokes (areas) will be neglected. That is OK in the short run. You may be starting a business, so the financial aspect is going down, not up. You may have a sick family member, so career or education is taking a back seat to other priorities. Short-term neglect is OK, but most people are actually practicing long-term neglect. Don't lie to yourself by thinking it is OK to continually neglect your health, not to work on getting out of debt, or not to work on healing broken relationships. Take action today; start now. Many times getting the spoke back in the wheel is painful, but it's always well worth it.

Be intentional. Start this month by setting a small goal for each area of your life. These small goals should be small steps to a larger goal. Post them on your mirror or other prominent place.

Faith

The center of the wheel is your soul. It is an open space to be filled by God, who created it. Many people treat their soul as a big hole, constantly trying to fill it with something. These people are always searching for something to give them lasting meaning, purpose or significance. It is like they are desperately trying to find life from a relationship or an activity. Any area of our life can be what we try to fill our soul with. We attempt to fill our soul with success, marriage, financial freedom, sports, clothes, recreation, new houses, cars or even Facebook. The sad thing is that it is never enough. God is the only one who can fill the soul completely, giving satisfaction and contentment, because our soul was designed for Him to fill. David wrote in the Psalms 73, *"Whom have I in heaven but you? And earth has nothing I desire besides you. My flesh and my heart may fail, but God is the strength of my heart and my portion forever."*

If you have never asked God to fill your soul, you can do it now. Jesus, God's only son, said in John 10: 10, *"The thief comes only to steal and kill and destroy; I have come that they may have life, and have it to the full."*

The Apostle Paul encouraged people with these words in Romans 10: 9, *"That if you confess with your mouth, 'Jesus is Lord,' and believe in your heart that God raised him from the dead, you will be saved."*

Begin today!

I read this _ _ _ _ _ _ times this week

Are You a Drifter? Wheel of Life, Part 2

This is a follow-up on the previous discussion about the wheel of life. Are you a drifter? There are two forms of drifting. The first form is when a boat is navigating a current in a river, heading for a fixed point on the other side. If the helmsman is not paying strict attention to the desired point, the current will push the boat downstream. The boat can still reach the desired point, but it now must be headed more directly into the current, and a much greater effort is required to reach the desired point.

The second type of drifting is where a boat is poorly moored to the dock. The current will tug at the lines and cause the boat to drift away from the dock, many times breaking free and floating downstream or going out with the tide.

It is easy to drift in life. We either are not paying strict attention to where we want to go and the current pushes us downstream, or we think we are securely fixed to strong values, but in actuality, we are poorly secured. Are you drifting in one or more areas of your life, even though you may be thinking, "The effort I am giving or have given is enough"?

- Finances – Is your spending out of control? Did you tell yourself, "This one more purchase on my credit card won't matter"?

- Family – Are you assuming everything is OK in your marriage or with your children, even though you have done nothing to strengthen your marriage or family relationships in the past month?

- Career – Do you do just enough to get by? Are you cutting corners at work? Have you been putting off going back to school or finding that new job?

- Health – Do you tell yourself, "My weight doesn't matter. I feel OK"? Or have you been procrastinating going for your annual checkup, thinking, "I feel fine"?

- Mental – Are you letting others reinforce their values by whatever you watch on TV, or are you consciously seeking out wholesome material that reinforces what you believe? Are you thinking, "This one book, movie, song or Internet site won't affect me"?

- Social/Cultural – Is there a relationship that needs healing but you have been putting off going to talk with the person? Are you taking the easy way out by not getting to know your neighbor or by not helping someone in need?

- Spiritual/Ethical – Are you letting others teach your children values? Or are you consciously leading your family in this area? Are you letting the culture's values slowly creep in and replace the things that you were taught and know are right?

Are you drifting?

Faith

Hebrews 2: 1 – *"We must pay more careful attention, therefore, to what we have heard so that we do not drift away."*

To quote my pastor, Bob Flayhart, "We need to carefully secure our lives to the gospel, or the cultural currents of life will cause us to slowly, quietly drift spiritually away."

The cause of spiritual drifting is that you are not consciously working to reinforce your spiritual values. There is no shortcut. Maintaining your spiritual course requires conscious effort; once a week is not enough.

Take action!

I read this _ _ _ _ _ _ _ times this week.

Leadership:
The Importance of
Goal-Setting

On Monday this week did you wake up with a clear focus or itinerary of what you were going to do this week or this month? Did you spend any time over the weekend or this morning planning out your week? Do you have any particular goals you want to accomplish this week or month, quarter or year? Too many people just get up each day and live for that day. They have no driving purpose, no meaning to life, except to get through the day. Are you one of these people? If so, that is when life is leading you.

A Life Leader sets goals, achieves them and continually makes new goals. These goals aren't just self-focused, either; many of them are others-focused.

The Power of Goals

To truly be motivated, to have purpose in your life, you need goals. Goals provide stimulation, creativity, motivation and purpose. Goals keep you from just focusing on the now, the moment and whatever you are dealing with at the time. Goals keep you looking forward. A goal is not a goal unless is it something that is tangible. You can have a subjective goal, but it must be measured by an objective goal. To form a goal, it needs to be **SMART** – **S**pecific, **M**easurable, **A**ttainable, **R**ealistic and **T**angible. The goal must have a timetable to when it is to be achieved. People who set goals but don't set specific ones or don't track (measure their success) in achieving their goal have difficulties in succeeding. These people say, "I tried goal-setting, and it didn't work." (No, they did not "work" to truly achieve the goal; they only *hoped* it would happen.)

If you are having trouble achieving your goals, then I suggest you look at the requirements of a goal and see if you have covered your entire basis in setting that goal. How specific is it? What are you using to measure your success? Can the measurement be broken down into smaller measurements? Is the goal attainable as you are today? Do you need to change something about yourself or circumstances to truly achieve this goal? Is the goal realistic for where you are in life? Is the goal tangible? If not, then find a tangible goal that will signify the intangible. Break the goal into smaller, achievable steps. It is OK to set high goals and difficult ones, but not ridiculous ones.

The point here is that without goals, you are a wondering generality. Whatever happens to you today will determine what you do tomorrow. A Life Leader does not allow the circumstances of today to control his or her tomorrows.

If you want to become an effective goal-setter, then search the topic goal setting on the web. There are a lot of writers on the subject.

Now, go set some goals!

Faith

The apostle Paul had a specific goal. He wrote about it in Philippians 3: 12-14 – *"Not that I have already obtained all this, or have already been made perfect, but I press on to take hold of that for which Christ Jesus took hold of me. Brothers, I do not consider myself yet to have taken hold of it. But one thing I do: Forgetting what is behind and straining toward what is ahead, I press on toward the goal to win the prize for which God has called me heavenward in Christ Jesus."*

That one goal of heaven and eternal life motivated him to set smaller, realistic tangible goals of getting the gospel to a specific city or writing a letter to a certain church.

Jesus had a goal of going to Jerusalem to die for everyone's sin. Jesus was motivated and would let nothing get in his way of going to the cross. He rebuked Peter in Matthew 16: 21-23 when Peter said to Jesus that he should not go up to Jerusalem and die.

"From that time on, Jesus began to explain to his disciples that he must go to Jerusalem and suffer many things at the hands of the elders, chief priests and teachers of the law, and that he must be killed and on the third day be raised to life. Peter took him aside and began to rebuke him. 'Never, Lord!' he said. 'This shall never happen to you!' Jesus turned and said to Peter, 'Get behind me, Satan! You are a stumbling block to me; you do not have in mind the things of God, but the things of men.'"

As you see, goals give purpose to our being, our life. Both Jesus and Paul had a primary goal (I call it their life goal), and around that goal all other goals were set. Do you have a life goal?

The Bible says our life goal is to glorify God. Knowing that, do all your other goals work toward that one goal? If not, ask God to change your focus, your purpose and your reason for living.

I read this _ _ _ _ _ _ _ times this week.

Discipline

If someone were describing you, would they use the word "disciplined"? What is discipline? The root word is "disciple" – the general meaning is to be a committed follower of a way, path or person. What way are you following? Life Leadership's foundation is discipline. It is having an understanding of a way or lifestyle one should follow, then following that path. It is saying "no" to many things so you can say "yes" to a few precious, valuable, life-sustaining things. Discipline is self-control. The majority of people see discipline as hindering their free expression or the pursuit of freedom. Actually, discipline frees a person to truly seek fulfillment and achieve the goals that have meaning. By disciplining yourself away from the unnecessary or the meaningless, you can achieve the meaningful.

The Mark of Discipline

A disciplined person doesn't just come home and carelessly watch TV. A disciplined person is careful in what he or she puts in his or her mind. A disciplined person knows that if he/she is not actively working on where he/she wants to go, he/she will be swept backward by the generalities of life. If you are not pushing forward, the generalities of life, the vices, the meaningless things are pushing you backwards. You are being controlled, not controlling.

Being disciplined takes several steps:

1. It is a conscious choice: "I will be different. I will think about how I live my life. I will make conscious choices that have a positive impact on me and others."

2. Discipline has an end in sight: a goal or an outcome or attitude, a benefit.

3. Discipline involves the realization that your choices affect other people, so you make choices and decisions with others in mind.

4. The disciplined person weighs the benefits of his or her discipline and continually verbally expresses the good results that this discipline brings.

5. A disciplined person makes of choice of "Do it now" vs. "That can wait until tomorrow," for tomorrow never comes.

6. A particular discipline practiced becomes a habit, freeing you to learn to be disciplined in other areas.

7. The number one underlying principle of all successful people is that they are disciplined in the area of their success.

Where a person struggles in life: work, physical fitness, marriage, finances, etc., the general cause is that the person was not or stopped being disciplined in this area. The person stopped working for a goal, stopped considering others and only lived for himself or herself, for the moment at hand, not the future. Live for the future, not just for today.

"I wish I was disciplined" is a common cop-out. What it means is that the goal that you wish you had is really not valuable enough for you to change. To be truly disciplined, you must first discipline your mind. In the words of Zig Ziglar, "You change what you are and where you are by changing what goes into your mind."

Faith

The apostle Paul understood discipline. He understood the temptations of the world and how simple distractions could keep him from doing the task that God had called him to do. He wrote in 1 Corinthians 9: 26-27, *"Therefore I do not run like a man running aimlessly; I do not fight like a man beating the air. No, I beat my body and make it my slave so that after I have preached to others, I myself will not be disqualified for the prize."*

in his book *Tough Minded Faith for Tender Hearted People* Dr. Robert Schuller states that there is power in discipline. (Faith is disciplining yourself to succeed. P. 130):

"The person who disciplines his body practices faith whether it's through controlling appetite for food or drink, or any other natural physical appetite. There are mysterious, intricate, and complex connections of body, brain and soul. Persons who discipline their eating, drinking and sexual appetites, often experience a mysterious upsurge of creative powers and rebirth of spirituality. In contrast, the undisciplined person who lets himself/herself go and doesn't care about proper exercise, physical fitness or a dietary discipline finds his faith becoming 'flabby.' 'Undisciplined' is another word for 'disqualified.'"

If you are struggling in your faith about God, His answering of your prayers, or other life problems, I would first examine your discipline in the area of faith and in life. What are you continually putting in your mind? Are you reading God's word on a daily basis? Are you fellowshipping with other believers on a regular basis? Do you attend church on a regular basis? Are you in a relationship that is unwholesome? Are you in a rut, but blaming others or God?

So many times, we look to others for an answer to our problems, but the answer is really about us. We are the solution, but the solution requires you or me making a change, being disciplined. God gives us the grace and spiritual power to change our lives, but He doesn't just "zap" us; we must exercise discipline in making those changes.

So start today!

I read this _ _ _ _ _ _ _ *times this week.*

Dealing with Pain, Part 1

Everyone in life will experience pain, whether emotional, physical or spiritual. The question is, "How will you deal with that pain?" Physically, pain is a good thing in warning us that there is something wrong. It is the same emotionally or spiritually.

In February 2004, I had rotator cuff surgery. It was a 4-year-old injury that kept getting worse until I could no longer manage the pain. So I had it fixed. The challenge was that I knew the recovery was going to be worse, in terms of pain, than the injury, but the long-term results were worth it. I can swim, kayak and, best of all, sleep again.

As with my injury, pain has stages. You first ignore it. Then you must consciously deal with it, but it is manageable. Third, you begin to look for ways to numb the pain, as with over-the-counter drugs like aspirin, Tylenol or Advil in the case of physical pain. As the pain lingers or increases, you look for stronger means of numbing; in the metaphor of physical pain, you use more over-the-counter remedies or go to a doctor and get stronger narcotic pain pills. Finally, when those numbing techniques do not work or you start to become reliant on them, you do whatever it takes to fix the problem. In the case of physical pain, you get surgery to fix the problem. Once the problem is fixed, you go through rehab and more short-term pain to become normal again.

Pain in Your Life

Do you have pain in your life? How are you dealing or coping with that pain? Depending on its severity, it should not be overlooked. Many times we just try to numb the pain with stronger painkillers, such as narcotics, alcohol, working harder, having an affair, not talking to the person or pretending it did not happen. Life Leaders know that just numbing the pain has long-term negative consequences. Life Leaders look at the pain and begin to address how to fix the problem that caused the pain. Life Leaders ask themselves, "What can I do to get beyond this pain?" or "How can I redeem this situation?"

Do I need to ask forgiveness of someone or address an offense?

Do I need to start loving my spouse, even though he/she doesn't deserve it?

Do I need to stop eating and start exercising?

Do I need to get out of a harmful relationship?

Do I need to get another job or change my behavior with my existing job?

Do I need to seek help to redeem a relationship or change a destructive habit?

Life Leaders identify the long-term benefits and work through the short-term pain to achieve the long-term results.

Faith

Isaiah 61: 1-3 – *"The Spirit of the Sovereign LORD is on me, because the LORD has anointed me to preach good news to the poor. He has sent me to bind up the brokenhearted, to proclaim freedom for the captives and release from darkness for the prisoners, to proclaim the year of the LORD's favor and the day of vengeance of our God, to comfort all who mourn, and provide for those who grieve in Zion – to bestow on them a crown of beauty instead of ashes, the oil of gladness instead of mourning, and a garment of praise instead of a spirit of despair. They will be called oaks of righteousness, a planting of the LORD for the display of his splendor."*

This is a prophecy of Jesus Christ. Jesus came to pay for our sins, to relieve our pain and to re-establish our relationship with God. Are you re-established?

Take action!

I read this _ _ _ _ _ _ _ times this week.

Dealing with Pain, Part 2

This is a sensitive issue and by no means fully covers the topic of pain. My focus is on the things that we do to cause pain or relieve pain.

Life is full of pain. Your response to pain will determine what type of life you lead, whether you acknowledge the fact that life is full of pain and then work to live within that fact or whether you work to protect yourself, preventing pain. Physical pain is generally caused by diseases or accidents. Spiritual pain is generally caused by sin and our lack of belief or purpose. Much emotional pain is caused by broken relationships or inappropriate relationships that lead in the wrong direction.

I recently heard a guy speak just after he had had a severe acid reflux problem surgically corrected. Right after surgery, his pain was gone. He commented that he had not realized how much of his life was spent managing his pain. How are you dealing with pain? Has your pain become so great that it defines who you are? How you deal with this pain will determine your future.

Life Leaders focus on the resolution of pain, not the mitigation of pain. Life Leaders don't spend the majority of time looking for ways to avoid or numb the pain, but instead focus on how to relieve or find a solution to and healing of the pain. In finding resolution, they realize that they can't change other people and how other people act. Instead of focusing the blame on others or circumstances, Life Leaders know that the only person they can change is themselves and therefore spend their energy on changing themselves for healing. This healing may come from counseling, trusting in God, restoring friendships, asking forgiveness or even getting in shape.

Life Leaders look at the 7 areas of their life: spiritual, social, mental, physical, financial, career, family. They ask themselves, "Is there something that I am doing or am not doing that is causing myself or someone else pain in one or all of these areas?"

Life Leaders routinely examine their lives to change themselves to bring healing. These people focus on the long-term results and are willing to go through the process (although it may be painful) to bring about a wholesome resolution. Life Leaders get help when needed and look to redeem a situation, no matter who is at fault.

Faith

In Luke 8, Jesus heals a woman who had suffered from bleeding for 12 years, and he also heals the Synagogue ruler's daughter.

Luke 8: 47 – *"Then the woman, seeing that she could not go unnoticed, came trembling and fell at his feet. In the presence of all the people, she told why she had touched him and how she had been instantly healed. Then he said to her, 'Daughter, your faith has healed you. Go in peace.'"*

And later, regarding the little girl – *"Hearing this, Jesus said to Jairus, 'Don't be afraid; just believe, and she will be healed.'"*

To be healed of our pain, we first must believe that Jesus Christ is God and that He can heal us. Are you suffering? Seek healing through Christ and with Christ, but first you must believe that you can be healed.

Believe today!

I read this _ _ _ _ _ _ times this week.

Motivation: Desire vs. Fear

Most people don't realize that it takes the same amount of energy to fear or worry about something as it does to desire and work toward a positive goal. Desire and fear are just two sides of a coin. If you are focused on negative things, flip the coin and focus on positive things. You get what you focus on – good or bad. Talk in positive terms, not negative. Focus on positive self-motivation, not negative. Speak in positive terms, such as "I can, I will" vs. "I'll try, I can't."

When you talk with others, speak in positive terms. Tell your children, co-workers or spouse what you want to happen, instead of what you don't want to happen. For instance, tell your spouse, "Please remember to stop by the store on the way home," instead of, "Don't forget to stop by the store." Put forth a positive, take-action thought rather than a negative, "don't do" thought.

To achieve your goals, focus on the specific things that need to be done and write them down. Read them as often as needed. Say them aloud. By doing this, you are putting the emphasis on what you desire. If you don't write them down and repeat them regularly, fear of the negative consequences can take over.

Success is one side of the coin and failure the other. What side are you looking at?

Faith

Colossians 3: 1-2 – *"Since, then, you have been raised with Christ, set your hearts on things above, where Christ is seated at the right hand of God. Set your minds on things above, not on earthly things."*

Whatever we place our affections on will control our hopes, dreams, attitudes, money and relationships. Not only do our affections need to be set on what is eternal, but our minds also need to be set on what is eternal, because, in life, the two cannot be separated. Therefore, set your mind on Christ, and other things will take their proper place.

As the mind thinks, so the heart becomes.

I read this _ _ _ _ _ _ _ times this week.

Entertainment- Are You Addicted?

Have you ever thought about Americans' obsession with entertainment? There are over 500 channels of TV, 24-hour news, DVDs, iPods, the Internet and talk radio, just to name a few. Americans act as if entertainment is a right guaranteed in the United States Constitution. But most people never ask the question, "Is all this entertainment good for me?" No, they just sit and watch TV or listen to the radio, even to the junk or filth that comes on. Many times the attitude is, "I must be entertained!" I have heard people say, "I know there is junk on the TV, but there is nothing else to watch."

The sad thing about entertainment is that the time spent watching TV could be spent building relationships, increasing your knowledge, helping your neighbor, getting in shape, or positively contributing to society. You get my point. Many just plop down on the couch, turn on the tube and check their brain and everything else on the shelf. Instead they could or should be asking, "What can I do today that will be beneficial to me and my family, my neighbors and my community?" Not only does mindless entertainment cost wasted time and opportunity, but it also causes people's minds to become lazy.

If you fit in this category, I suggest that for two weeks, you not watch TV and instead read a positive book, work in the yard, visit with your family or neighbor, or complete a project around the house.

The point is, do something that will benefit you, not just something to help you exist. Use your car CD player as your school. Instead of listening to the radio, listen to a motivational CD or positive music. (The links I have on my website, www.mindspring.com/~billhart, are great resources for such things.) Apply this to your kids, also; have them take a break from video games, TV, the Internet and other mind-numbing electronics.

To help me battle the desire to watch the tube all the time, I set a goal to read 20 books per year. I keep score on a chart so I know where I am. It was tough last December with all the bowl games on and I had two books to go. Some of the books on my list are the ones my kids are reading. Not only is this beneficial to my mind and attitude, but it is also a great way to stay engaged with my kids.

Faith

Philippians 4: 8-9 – *"Finally, brothers, whatever is true, whatever is noble, whatever is right, whatever is pure, whatever is lovely, whatever is admirable; if anything is excellent or praiseworthy; think about such things. Whatever you have learned or received or heard from me, or seen in me; put it into practice. And the God of peace will be with you."*

This is the Apostle Paul encouraging you to focus on what is positive, valuable and meaningful. In order to think about things that are excellent, praiseworthy and life-changing, you must stop allowing popular entertainment to put junk into your mind.

As the old adage says, "You become what you think." Or, as Zig Ziglar says, "You are what you are because of what goes into your mind. You change what you are and where you are by changing what goes into your mind."

Do you want to really become like the TV shows? I hope not. Make a choice today to change what you put into your mind!! Take charge of your life and be different!

I read this _ _ _ _ _ _ _ times this week.

Do You Muse?

It is amazing how much energy is spent on being amused. The word "muse" means to think. "Amuse" means *not* thinking. We have become a society of non-thinkers. Movies have a camera angle change every 1 second to keep our attention. Commercials are short, fast-moving and very shallow. Political points are made in 30-second sound bites. We have become a society who asks for less, not more, in terms of stimulating thought.

I believe the continual pursuit of entertainment or amusement is very detrimental to a person and society. The problem with entertainment is that it is self-focused, not others-focused. The statement "I'm bored" shows two things about the speaker: 1) He or she is focusing on self, and 2) He or she is focused on being entertained or amused versus being productive.

Being entertained is different from playing. As children or adults play, it requires thinking, social interaction and a purpose. Playing builds skills in creative thinking, motor coordination, conflict resolution, imagination, determination, goals and many other crucial life lessons. Entertainment does none of the above. Playing can build character and skills. Do you focus more on entertaining your kids or making them play? Can your kids ride in the car without watching a DVD? Be careful in how you train your kids; you could make them addicted to entertainment.

Our society accepts many of the problems today with an "Oh well, it will just happen" attitude. In general, society has become lazy, focused on self instead of focused on making a difference. Life Leaders take the opposite approach, saying, "I can work for the betterment of society by beginning at home."

TV during the week is greatly limited in our house. It is "amazing" what our kids are doing in place of TV. They are doing what kids used to do before TV, video games and the Internet; they read or practice their musical instrument. They go out and play with the neighbors. Both kids are now into jump-roping and other physical fitness activities. When we have limited their *amusement*, they *muse* in many ways.

Pursuing amusement is an attitude; so is musing. What characterizes your family? Yourself?

Faith

Ecclesiastes 6: 11 – *"Sow your seed in the morning, and at evening let not your hands be idle, for you do not know which will succeed, whether this or that, or whether both will do equally well."*

2 Thessalonians 3: 6 – *"In the name of the Lord Jesus Christ, we command you, brothers, to keep away from every brother who is idle and does not live according to the teaching you received from us."*

As the old saying goes, "An idle mind is the devil's workshop."

We are warned about being idle, especially in the evening. Ecclesiastes says there is a time and season for all things. Too many times we focus on the time of work during the day and are idle in the evening. Instead, in the evening we could be building relationships, stimulating our minds, building family, exercising, planning or even resting and getting the needed sleep.

The evening time gives us the opportunity to focus on other areas of our life besides work, such as building our marriage, spending time with the family, doing a project at home or even helping a neighbor.

Take action in your family – let change begin today!

I read this _ _ _ _ _ _ _ times this week.

Purpose

Do you have purpose in your life? Most people spend their life trying to find their purpose. For most people, purpose lies right in front of their nose, and they don't see it. Your purpose is what really motivates you down deep. Your purpose will be about helping others in some way.

What keeps us from believing we really have a purpose or pursuing that purpose are circumstances and attitudes. We see the obstacles as greater or more powerful than the cause. We believe our comfort is more important than our purpose. We see the darkness and how big it is and think, "I can never conquer that."

A favorite quote of Eleanor Roosevelt's was, "Better to light a candle than curse the darkness." A candle does not eliminate all darkness, but it does light the area around you. It gives you enough light to do something.

You can choose today to be a part of the solution, not part of the problem. You will find purpose in the projects you support.

Faith

Matthew 5: 13-16 – *"You are the salt of the earth. But if the salt loses its saltiness, how can it be made salty again? It is no longer good for anything, except to be thrown out and trampled by men.*

You are the light of the world. A city on a hill cannot be hidden. Neither do people light a lamp and put it under a bowl. Instead they put it on its stand, and it gives light to everyone in the house. In the same way, let your light shine before men, that they may see your good deeds and praise your Father in heaven."

As believers, God has given us a purpose, which is to bring praise to the Father in heaven. He has given each person a purpose or dream in how he or she is to serve God.

In my life, God has challenged me to look beyond circumstances or comfort to see where He is calling me to shine the light. Many times it's tough, but it is always rewarding and fulfilling. One area that I ignored God's calling for 3 years was serving inner-city children at Cornerstone Schools of Alabama. My excuse was that it was downtown, way too far to drive, and I did not have the time.

I finally heeded God's call and have found such significance and purpose in serving those kids that I now joyfully drive the 18 miles and block time to serve. It is amazing that once I started, the drive was not really that far, and I can easily find the time to serve.

As you shine your light where God has called you and enabled you, you will find purpose.

A great book to read is *Dream Giver* by Bruce Wilkinson. It is short and tells a story of a guy named Ordinary pursuing his dream. You and your kids will enjoy it.

Start today!

I read this _ _ _ _ _ _ _ times this week.

Pursuing Excellence vs. Perfectionism

Have you ever been around a person who is never satisfied until the job or the performance is perfect? It appears that perfectionists are fixated on getting the project just right at the expense of people's feelings or other priorities. Are you that type of person? Perfectionism is a bad habit. It typically stems from low confidence or a fear of failure or combination of the two. Many people are perfectionists because they are more pre-occupied with what others *might* think about them than with finding out what others really *do* think about them. They are self-absorbed and see things only from their perspective looking out, not what others see of them from the outside looking in.

Perfectionists are typically:

-Critical
-Harried and time-crunched
-Unable to see the big picture
-Stressed
-Unconfident
-Rarely, if ever, inclined to allow a sense of true accomplishment and personal reward

Perfectionists are typically no fun to be around. The one true observation about a perfectionist is that he or she is typically not involved in self-improvement. You don't see a perfectionist regularly challenging his/her own assumptions. He or she typically doesn't read a lot on leadership, goal-setting and learning how to serve others. Perfectionists, in many ways, are very self-centered.

True leaders focus on excellence instead of perfection. Excellence is the focus on the end result – "Did my action meet, satisfy or accomplish the desired goal?" Excellence is others-focused as well as outcome-focused. Perfectionists rank the particulars of the process (doing it their way) as high as the outcome. In work, perfectionists typically micro-manage and focus on conformity versus allowing people to work according to their strengths.

The person concentrating on excellence has a mindset of:

-Continual growth and learning
-Satisfaction of a job well done and clients served
-Flexibility and adaptability
-Satisfaction, due to an ability to complete things and move on
-Lower stress, thanks to clarified expectations
-Strong sense of meaningful accomplishment

Choose today to be a person pursuing excellence versus perfection.

Excerpts from: http://www.refresher.com/!jswmindset.html
Maintaining a Mindset of Excellence, by Jamie S. Walters

Faith

Have an understanding that you will never reach perfection until heaven. This frees you to pursue the more important things in life. When you understand that God does not demand perfection from us, then you are freed to learn what God really does desire from us.

The reason God does not demand perfection from us is that we cannot be perfect because of sin. God had a remedy for the sin problem before He even created the world. In Ephesians 1 the Apostle Paul wrote that through Christ, *"We are chosen to be holy and blameless (perfect) in His (God's) sight before the creation of the world."*

This perfection is obtained through faith in Jesus Christ. God does require perfection. Jesus met those requirements by living a perfect life, then dying for the sins of the world (yours and mine). His death was to cover our imperfection. Our requirement in being perfect is to have faith in the perfect sacrifice, Jesus Christ, to save us from our sins. God says that Jesus is our substitute in meeting His requirement.

So if God does not require perfection in us on earth, what does He require? He requires a life of continual transformation for His glory, setting your mind and life on living for Him.

I read this _ _ _ _ _ _ _ times this week.

Courage

Short-Term vs. Long-Term Decision-Making

American culture conditions us to make decisions based on the short term, or the need for immediate results. Our culture does not teach us to look at the long-term implications of our actions, as many other societies do. We are even encouraged by the media and advertising to do it now. "Buy now," "Please yourself" or "No one waits until they're married" are good examples. This is evidenced in teen sex, obesity, divorce, disobedient children and in the fact that so many people are in excessive debt. Getting in debt, especially credit card debt, is a system of short-term decision-making. Even in the corporate world, short-term "decision making" is a problem. Publicly traded American companies are judged on quarterly profits, not long-term gains. Therefore, executives make decisions based upon what will boost short-term profits, not long-term growth. In the long run, the company is hurt by not spending money to improve or replace equipment, and/or the company downsizes and loses long-term market share or profits.

Are You a Short-Termer?

As a person, is your life guided by the short-term benefit of decision-making? Are you in debt? Are you overweight? Are you compromising your morals? Are there things in your life that you have been putting off because it is uncomfortable to address the issue or relationship? Are you making poor decisions, based only upon a short-term perspective, to avoid doing something uncomfortable now? The long-term decision is most beneficial, but it is uncomfortable to make.

Be Courageous

It takes courage to ask yourself, "What are the long-term consequences of this short-term decision?" Most people live their lives without ever asking such questions. They hope that they will never have to "pay the piper" for short-term living. But in reality, everyone must "pay the piper." If you have goals for your life, these goals enable you to ask yourself, "Will this short-term decision benefit my long-term goals?" Specific goals help you see the long run, not just the immediate "I want this....whatever." Goals help you have courage to say "no" to how other people live their lives so you can live your life achieving *your* goals, not a credit card company's or some advertiser's goals. Long-term goals can keep you out of trouble.

Faith

It takes courage in faith to decide to stand for what is right. Deciding to be different takes faith, for the long-term benefits outweigh the short-term "costs." Practicing moral behavior when your friends aren't takes faith – faith that God's word says you will benefit yourself by not participating in such behavior.

Faith is all about long-term decisions, from where you place your affections to where you will spend eternity. When asked about eternity – heaven or hell – too many people say, "I will decide that later." In making that short-term decision ("Don't bother me with that now"), they are actually developing a long-term decision also. For many, there won't be a choice or opportunity in the long term, for the short-term decision becomes a long-term habit of not addressing the long-term issues.

Where will you be in eternity – heaven or hell? It is a long-term decision.

I read this _ _ _ _ _ _ _ times this week.

Changing or Adjusting Your Attitude in Hard Times

I have heard many people say, "Attitude is everything." Attitude does determine how one approaches any situation. Attitude is made up of your past experiences and the predominant thoughts in your mind. If our past experiences were negative, or always risk-averse, our predominant thoughts will have a tendency to be jaded or cynical. A person can't change his or her past, but he or she can change the future. Many outside forces that act upon us can't be changed, but how we respond is a huge factor in determining what happens next. A positive attitude is the first determinant in being a Life Leader. A positive attitude for a Life Leader does several things: 1) It enables him/her to see more clearly during the tough times or to look for the silver lining.   2) It gives hope for the future. 3) It causes a person to work for the future. 4) It enables a person to look to associate with others who have a positive attitude. 5) It combats all the negative thoughts, experiences, etc. that a negative world throws at the person. (It basically insulates a person.) 6) A positive attitude enables a person to look at himself or herself and ask, "What do I need to do to change?" Many times it is we who need to change to make the circumstances better, not vice versa.

In hard times a positive attitude does not necessarily reduce the severity of the hardship, but it enables a person to get through the difficult time in one piece, so to speak. A positive attitude also positively affects those who the Life Leader comes into contact with: family, friends, co-workers, even strangers.

Developing a Positive Attitude: Thoughts and Actions

How does one develop a positive attitude? It is developed in primarily two ways: our thought-life and our actions. For our thought-life, consider: 1) What do you constantly put into your mind? Do you allow just about anything to go into your mind (the thought of *amusing* versus *musing*), or do you consciously seek positive input, such as positive music, books, people, etc.? 2) How do you talk to yourself and to others? 3) Do you speak in positive terms or negative terms? "I can do that" or "It can't be done." "That person is a jerk" vs. "That person needs help or is having a bad day." Do you focus on what you should do or shouldn't do in your conversation? Do you say, "Don't forget... (a negative thought)" vs. "Remember to... (a positive thought)"? Do you say more "no" than "yes"?

To have a positive attitude, positive thoughts must replace negative thoughts. You can't just get rid of negative thoughts; they must be REPLACED. Your mind can't handle a vacuum. To remove something bad, it must be replaced with something good.

The second method for developing a positive attitude is minding our actions. Our actions determine our attitude. 1) Body language – how you walk or stand. Do you walk with your head up, eyes straight ahead, or do you walk bent over with your eyes to the ground? 2) When greeting or meeting with someone, look that person in the eye when you talk – greet him or her and specifically look him or her in the eye; give that person a warm handshake. 3) Tone of voice – force yourself to speak in a positive tone. By doing things that look positive, your body will begin to adjust the attitude of the mind. The body and mind must always be in synch. So if you force the body to be positive, the mind will be also. If you force the mind to be positive, your body will follow.

Faith

Jeremiah 33: 3 – *"Call to me and I will answer you and show you great and mighty things which you do not know."*

God wants us to have a positive attitude developed through faith in him. He has made us promises in Romans 8: 28 that whatever happens to a Christian is for the Christian's good, whether we can understand that or not. If you are suffering from a negative attitude, ask God to change it. Focus on the future, and allow God to change your attitude toward your past. He can heal you of your pain and enable you to have a positive attitude, to be forgiven, to walk in His love, to move forward. Your present circumstances can be extremely negative, but your attitude does not have to be that way. Call to God; He can change you. Get into God's word and search for His promises, those "great and mighty things which you do not know." Memorize those promises and replace the negative thoughts with these promises. I put such verses on 3x5 cards to study and memorize. I generally place them on my car dashboard so I can read them anytime I am in the car.

Some helpful verses are: Philippians 4: 4-9; Philippians 4: 13, 19; Romans 8: 1-3, 37-38; Psalms 40; Psalms 119: 92-93; Psalms 27: 14; Isaiah 40: 28-31; Isaiah 41: 10; Isaiah 57: 13, 2nd half of the verse.

Get started today!

I read this _ _ _ _ _ _ _ times this week.

How to Say "I Love You" and Mean It

Have you ever done something that you thought another person would really enjoy, but he/she seemed ungrateful or not impressed? Have you ever gone out of your way and expected a "Thanks a lot!" or "I appreciate what you did," but never received it? We all have. One of the most likely reasons the person did not respond was that you were not speaking his or her "love language." According to the book *The Five Languages of Love* by Gary Chapman, people have 1-2 primary ways that they like to be shown that you love, appreciate or care for them. The way or method is what Gary calls their "love language." If something is done for them outside of their love language, they don't appreciate or understand it. It does not register as something important to them.

The 5 love languages are:

1) Quality time – spending undivided time with someone where you can both connect; having meaningful time where relationship is affirmed.

2) Physical touch – a hug, kiss, or something that is physical. This is not romantic or sexual; for example, kids love to wrestle, women will give each other a hug, and men will give other guys a high five or a pat on the back.

3) Words of encouragement – telling someone how well he/she did or how special he/she is. Give positive, specific words, specifically emphasizing that person's value.

4) Acts of service – doing something for another, especially when it requires going out of your way.

5) Gift-giving – remembering someone by means of a gift. The gift, large or small, says, "I was thinking of you and bought this for you."

Changing for Others

The challenge with love languages is that you or I generally prefer both to be shown love or concern in our language, and to give that love or concern in our own preferred language. That works fine if both giver and recipient prefer gift-giving or quality time. But what happens when the giver prefers receiving words of encouragement and therefore gives words of encouragement, but the receiver prefers acts of service? There is a communication or "love" breakdown. One is attempting to show love, and yet the other is not receiving love. So no matter how hard you try giving words of encouragement, those words mean little to the receiver who would appreciate having things done for him or her – in this example, an act of service.

For instance, my primary love language is words of encouragement, and my wife's is acts of service. If I tell her, "Great job with the kids" or dinner or other thing but never "do" anything for her, she is not feeling "loved." If I clean the dishes or take her car to get fixed or clean the garage, she then feels loved. In her words, I showed her my love by doing something for her to express my appreciation. However, if she never says "thank you" or tells me that I did a great job of cleaning the garage, she is not speaking my love language, and I don't feel appreciated. Speaking different love languages is a major cause of marital conflict or even conflict in the workplace.

The Platinum Rule

A Life Leader learns another's love language and speaks that person's language to show appreciation. The Life Leader is not concerned about what he or she is comfortable doing to show love, but how the receiver knows he or she is loved or appreciated. The Life Leader changes his or her behavior in showing appreciation or love to meet the other person's need. **It is the Platinum rule – "Do to others as they would have you do to them."**

In the Workplace

For example, a manager, when rewarding a person for excellent performance, doesn't say, "Well, I don't like buying gifts, so I am not going to get them gift certificates to show my appreciation. I will buy them a plaque saying 'Job well done,' because I would want people to know how I performed." The good manager does his or her best to find out what the top performer's love language is and rewards according to that person's love language. If it is gift-giving, show appreciation with a gift card; if quality time, send him off with his spouse for a nice dinner; if acts of service... you get the idea. A Life Leader is concerned about others and adjusts his or her behavior for the benefit of others.

56

Faith

Jesus said that the second greatest commandment is to *"Love your neighbor as yourself."* Learning another's love language and speaking that language is doing just that. Adjusting your behavior to meet another's need for appreciation is truly loving your neighbor as yourself.

We all want to be loved or appreciated in our own love language. If we are stubborn or unwilling to learn what makes a person feel loved or appreciated, then we are self-centered and not living a life of faith. If you need to change to show a person you really care, ask God to help you to change. You can learn another's love language, and you can change your behavior to meet that person's need. Ask God. The apostle Paul wrote in Philippians 4: 13, *"I can do all things through Christ who strengthens me."* Well, so can you. Now, go love your spouse, kids, co-worker, parents and neighbor in their own language.

For more on this topic, I suggest you purchase Gary Chapman's book *The Five Languages of Love.*

I read this _ _ _ _ _ _ _ times this week.

Motivation -
Belief as the Foundation,
Part 1

Do you ever struggle with motivation? Have you ever tried to get your kids, co-workers or employees motivated about something, and they just don't get it? The first key to motivation is belief. People don't get motivated to do something unless they believe it is attainable and there is sufficient benefit for them to give the effort.

I am on the board of an inner-city Christian school that runs from K4 to 8th grade. The majority of students fall below the poverty line. Our academics are very rigorous, and the students achieve SAT scores equivalent to some of the top schools in the state. The majority of the 8th graders go on to 9th grade in a magnet school or some high-level private school on scholarship. Last year, 12 out of 16 made it to a top-level high school. I asked myself why the other 4 did not achieve that success. Every opportunity was given them to achieve. I know family situations and other problems greatly affect the students, but almost all these kids have the same life problems. I believe the fundamental problem of low achievement was that these 4 kids weren't personally motivated to achieve.

Believing is Seeing

This lack of personal motivation means that: 1) they did not believe that they could achieve the higher level or 2) they did not see the personal benefit. Knowing these kids, I think the first issue was the problem. To be sure that people believe they can achieve a goal, the goals first must be personal, owned by the person who needs to achieve. ("What will achieving this goal do for me?") Without personal buy-in, they won't be motivated to achieve. Then the goal must be broken down into believable and tangible steps. These steps also must be attainable. So, as a board member, I am now working on a program to help the kids set goals in small, tangible steps. I am working on them "owning" their success, not just their parents "making" them achieve. To help with this, I am bringing in successful African-American men and women to talk with the kids about achieving success. This will hopefully demonstrate to the kids that others succeeded, and so can they.

Getting Motivated

Are you having trouble being motivated to do something? If so, look at your belief. Do you see the benefit? Do you believe you can achieve it? If not, address both issues by setting tangible goals and listing expected benefits. Look for examples of others and how they succeeded. Investigate how others have overcome obstacles and stayed motivated in hard times. Teach these principles to your kids. As a family, set some goals and work together to achieve them.

Faith

Belief determines our success. In Joshua, God made a promise to the Israelites that He would give them all the land of Canaan that He had previously promised. This land was already occupied by a fierce people. God encouraged Joshua to "Be strong and courageous." Joshua had to believe God's promises to motivate himself to act. God encouraged Joshua to believe that Israel would take the land. Joshua did believe he could achieve what God had promised, and he clearly saw the benefit. Joshua led the people for 7 years, conquering the land. He was successful.

Joshua 1: 1-7 – *"After the death of Moses the servant of the LORD, the LORD said to Joshua son of Nun, Moses' aide: 'Moses my servant is dead. Now then, you and all these people, get ready to cross the Jordan River into the land I am about to give to them – to the Israelites. I will give you every place where you set your foot, as I promised Moses. Your territory will extend from the desert to Lebanon, and from the great river, the Euphrates – all the Hittite country – to the Great Sea on the west. No one will be able to stand up against you all the days of your life. As I was with Moses, so I will be with you; I will never leave you nor forsake you. Be strong and courageous, because you will lead these people to inherit the land I swore to their forefathers to give them. Be strong and very courageous.'"*

If you lack motivation, ask God to help you believe by seeing the benefit and by breaking the challenge into tangible and obtainable steps.

I read this _ _ _ _ _ _ _ times this week

Motivation, Part 2 –
Affirmation and Visualization

Are you having trouble believing you can achieve? Is guilt, fear or obligation the only thing that is motivating you? "I need to lose 10 pounds" or "I should go do that" or "I must work to pay the bills." "What will someone think of me if I don't do that or if I fail?" We are what we are because of what we think. Change your thinking. Start focusing on the things you want to do and the benefits of achieving those successes. You actually can create motivation where there is none. Our attitudes are created through repetitive thought. So to change an attitude, desire or habit, we need to change our repetitive thoughts.

Changing Your Thoughts

You change your thoughts by putting new thoughts into your mind in two ways: 1) affirmation 2) visualization. Affirmations are present-tense, positive statements about your new attitude or behavior. For instance, "I work out for 30 minutes each day." "I am a top performer." "I love my wife and show that love by telling her or doing things for her." "I encourage my kids daily." "I am a positive person." The key is present tense "I am" or "I do" vs. "I am going to do." As your subconscious mind hears what you say, your conscious mind will start believing what you are saying and take action to get "in-line" with the subconscious mind.

Successful affirmations are repeated to yourself at least once a day. I put mine on a 3x5 card and tape it to the bathroom mirror or keep an affirmation card on my dashboard in the car. Repetition is the key. If you only read affirmations a few times, your attitude and behavior won't change. It generally takes a minimum of twenty-one days of repeating the affirmation for it to become fixed in your mind. Affirmations need to be read out loud. When your ear hears you say it, your brain receives it as a truth. For that reason it is also important not to talk to yourself in a negative way, such as, "I knew I would fail." "I am a loser." "I can't," etc. Use affirmations on others; talk positively to your wife, kids, neighbors and co-workers.

Visualization is the process of rehearsing an attitude, behavior or desired outcome in your mind. You literally picture yourself being that way or doing the task or achieving the goal. To visualize, you practice in your mind the outcome you desire. When I go on a sales call, I picture the person saying "yes" to me. When I kayak, I picture in my mind how I am going to run the rapids down the river. I even picture myself saying loving things to my wife and her giving me a big hug. Visualize the benefits! If you don't see it in your mind, you can't see it in reality.

Your mind operates off whatever you put into it. So put positive thoughts into your mind. By putting these repetitive thoughts into your mind, you will tell your mind to work to achieve these results.

Faith

Back to Joshua – God used repetition in talking with Joshua to ensure his attitude and belief was in line with what God wanted. God told Joshua several times, *"Be strong and courageous."*

Also, God told Joshua and the people to meditate on His word, the Book of the Law. He told them to meditate on it day and night so that they would do what it says. In a way, God was saying, "Use my word as an affirmation and visualization. By doing so, you will do what I desire, and you will receive the blessing I promised."

God is commanding His people to read the word repetitively, not just one time, for attitudes and actions come from what we believe. What we believe comes from what we put in our brains. Character is formed through repetition, and so is motivation.

Joshua 1: 6-9 – *"Be strong and courageous, because you will lead these people to inherit the land I swore to their forefathers to give them. Be strong and very courageous. Be careful to obey all the law my servant Moses gave you; do not turn from it to the right or to the left, that you may be successful wherever you go. Do not let this Book of the Law depart from your mouth; meditate on it day and night, so that you may be careful to do everything written in it. Then you will be prosperous and successful. Have I not commanded you? Be strong and courageous. Do not be terrified; do not be discouraged, for the LORD your God will be with you wherever you go."*

I read this _ _ _ _ _ _ _ times this week

Motivation, Part 3 - Goal-Setting and Getting Back on Track

Once you are motivated to achieve because you believe you can achieve, it is time to set some specific goals.

Please review *The Importance of Goal-Setting* chapter (P. 21) for the details on how to set goals. One of the struggles in goal setting is one that I have heard people say: "I tried that, and it failed." Did the process fail, or did you fail? If the process was done correctly – that is, if the goals were specific, measurable, attainable, realistic and tangible, then what you most likely lacked was motivation. To become motivated, add these steps in the goal-setting process: 1) clearly define the benefit 2) add affirmations 3) add visualization of achievement where you imagine yourself enjoying the benefits.

Where Are You Now?

It is now Spring, and many of you set New Year's resolutions. Many of you started this year afresh, telling (affirming) yourself that last year was behind; you could start anew. Many of you needed to forgive yourself, or you needed to ask forgiveness of another to start this year correctly. How are you doing? Are you struggling? Are you in the midst of accomplishing your goals? Are you facing obstacles?

I am facing severe obstacles in accomplishing my business goals. Where the goal is big and the obstacles are many, my motivation must be great, my attitude must be strong, and I must have a very clear picture of the desired outcome and its benefits. I keep the outcome and benefits written on a white board in my office. Every time I get discouraged, I read those words and visualize the positive outcome. It motivates me to try harder.

Getting Back on Track

If you have become bogged down with your New Year goals or resolutions, go back and read (or write them down for the first time) the benefits of your goals. Picture yourself achieving them. Tell yourself how good you will feel, and imagine that feeling of accomplishment. Actually take some time, stop what you are doing, and imagine that you have accomplished the goal. Imagine how good you feel. Visualize your success. Now, get re-motivated. Create and use your affirmations to change your attitude and work toward those goals! You are a Life Leader; Life Leaders may get knocked down, but we get back up!

Faith

I have been studying King David in I and II Samuel. This man had his ups and downs. He was a good leader at times and a very poor leader at other times. He obeyed God in some areas, but greatly disobeyed God in others. Because of his disobedience, he suffered the consequences, and so did his family and the people of Israel.

With all David's failures, how could God say that David was a man after His own heart? God could say that because David was a man of repentance. When David saw his sin, he confessed his sin to God; he repented, and then worked to make things right, seeking God's guidance and strength. David got back on track with his relationship to God.

Did you have good intentions to have a solid relationship with God this year? Was your goal to have a quiet time, read the Bible more, go to church, or to help others? But have you messed up? If so, be like David – repent and get back on track. Ask God to help you.

I read this _ _ _ _ _ _ _ times this week.

Making Time Count

Some people count their time. Others make their time count!!!

Let's look at five ways to make your time count.

1. Love people and use money. Love may not make the world go 'round, but it sure makes the ride worthwhile! All of us should do a better job of embracing our most important relationships. Yet some of us are too focused on making money rather than on developing long-lasting, loving relationships. It was once said that money is a terrible master, but it is an excellent servant. Put people and money in the proper perspective.

2. Celebrate the *present time* in your life. Stay in the *here and now*. Another way of stating this is that you should enjoy the journey, not just the destination. Don't miss out on the positive, meaningful aspects of your daily life. Enjoy meeting those new customers. Celebrate your family's victories during the week.

3. Forgive and forget the past. All of us have regrets in our lives. However, we should avoid negative self-talk of "I should have..." or "If only I would have...." These negative thoughts waste a lot of time. Use the FIMO method to combat this: Forget It, Move Onward. Yesterday really did end last night. Today is a new day – made especially for you!

4. Find your positive motivation. We are all motivated, both positively and negatively. One definition of motivation is "a motive for action." Find what motivates you to take action and to invest your time in family, church or your hobby. Invest your time in those things that are important to you and that truly benefit you. Entertainment can be important to you, but does it really always benefit you?

5. Invest in yourself! You are the greatest asset you possess. In life, successful people never graduate from learning in all 7 areas of their life: marriage/family, career, finances, health, social/cultural, spiritual/ethical, and mental/educational. Therefore, you must invest in yourself. Personal growth precedes professional growth. Invest more in yourself than you do in your career.

   Well, there you have it. Each of these five ways will make your time count.

Faith

Ecclesiastes 3: 1 – *"There is a time for everything, and a season for every activity under heaven."*

Everyone's life has a season from youth to maturity, from school to career, from being single to marriage, from kids to empty-nesters, or maybe from low earning capacity to high earning capacity. Where are you in this season? Have you completed a season, and is it now a time for change? Do you have a plan for the change? Do you have a plan that goes beyond yourself?

Everyone has a dream, a God-given vision of how to make a difference in his or her life and in other people's lives. Is now the time for you to stop procrastinating and start pursuing your dream? Is there something in your life that now is the time for you to begin doing, but you need to stop doing something else first?

How do you treat time? Do you make it count for God's use, or do you just count time from your own perspective?

I read this _ _ _ _ _ _ _ times this week.

How Do You Talk?

Knowing that our attitude is what it is because of what goes into our mind, how do you talk to yourself, and how to you talk to others? You talk to yourself all day long, but the question is, in what context? Do you say positive or negative things to yourself? Do you say negative or positive things to others? One trait of all winners is that they talk to themselves in a positive manner. Typically, negative people or people who are failures do just the opposite.

Positive Talk = Positive Behavior

Parents, how do you talk to your children when you want them to do something? Do you tell them, "Don't play in the street" or "Stay in the yard"? Do you know the difference? Staying in the yard is the outcome you desire. If you said the first one, what you told them was actually to go into the street. Our minds can't visualize *not* doing something. When we are told not to do something, we see ourselves doing it, then tell ourselves, "I am not supposed to do that."

When you want your children to exhibit good behavior, tell them to do that good behavior, not to stop doing the bad behavior. For instance, "Johnny, don't pick on your sister" is not effective, because there is no desired outcome. The better answer is "Johnny, be kind to your sister." Being kind to his sister is the desired outcome.

The same principle applies in how you talk to your spouse, friends and employees. Focus on the desired result, not the undesired result. Say "Remember to..." versus "Don't forget to...."

How You Talk to Yourself

Self-talk is the same way. Talk to yourself in a positive context. Tell yourself that you are the type of person you want to be. Affirm yourself. Eliminate negative talk. "I am a winner." "I achieve my goals." "I am a friendly person." "I have a purpose in life."

You can also give affirmations to others. I tell my children almost every day that they are winners and that I love them. I tell them they can succeed, and, "When the going gets tough, the tough get going." We directly affect others in how we talk. Do you talk positively or negatively? Spend the next week focusing on positive talk, and see how it affects others.

Another question is, "Do you make statements or ask questions to communicate your ideas or position on an issue?" Making absolute statements, in many cases, is offensive to the other person. Asking a question to get to the same conclusion is much more palatable and not offensive to the receiver. An example of a statement is "That's impossible!" whereas a better way to handle that is to ask, "Why do you think that will work or is true?" A question is much less offensive than just telling someone your opinion.

Faith

Ephesians 4: 29-32 – *"Do not let any unwholesome talk come out of your mouths, but only what is helpful for building others up according to their needs, that it may benefit those who listen. And do not grieve the Holy Spirit of God, with whom you were sealed for the day of redemption. Get rid of all bitterness, rage and anger, brawling and slander, along with every form of malice. Be kind and compassionate to one another, forgiving each other, just as in Christ God forgave you."*

The Bible talks about wholesome talk for the same reason as listed above. What we think or talk about, we then become. Our thinking and talking determine who we are and also who others are. Jesus told us to love our neighbors as ourselves. One of the ways we do that is by the words we speak to ourselves and to each other. If we are continually talking negatively to ourselves, we will be negative toward others. If we talk down about ourselves, we will reflect or give that attitude to another. No person is an island; what you think directly affects you and directly or indirectly affects others.

Be positive; be encouraging!

I read this _ _ _ _ _ _ _ times this week.

How Well Do You Listen?

Most of us like to talk, especially to hear our opinions, thoughts or experiences. Even the most introverted person will talk when you address a subject about which he or she is passionate. I know I like to talk, but do I really listen? Recently I heard a sales training tape on listening, which caused me to start observing the art and skill of listening and how well I apply it and others apply it. Most of us do a poor job.

The Key Elements of Listening

Listening is all about relationships, for a good listener is truly interested in the other person. Before I go into what good listening is, I want to cover what good listening is not. Just being silent while the other person is talking is not a being good listener. Jumping onto one word the person said and then commenting on it is not good listening. Just saying "Uh huh" or "OK," "Yes, dear" or "Whatever you say" is poor listening. Good listening is not merely allowing the person to completely finish what they wanted to say before you speak.

I was a good example of a poor listener last week when my daughter was trying to explain why she wanted to do something. I heard what she said and even parroted it back, but I was not really hearing her feelings, emotions and motivations. I was not holding her thoughts as valuable in our relationship. I just wanted her to get to her point, and then I could speak.

Good Listening

Good listening requires attitude and skills. Here are the basic components of good listening:

1) Caring/willingness
The first premise of good listening is that you must want to listen or have a willingness to listen. This means you must truly have an interest in the other person and what he or she has to say. Willingness means that you want not only to hear, but you

also want or desire to understand. At the heart of listening is the attitude of caring, compassion and humility.

2) Ability

The second part of effective listening is ability. Ability means you need to focus, not on yourself or what you will say next, but on what the other person is truly saying, not just the words that are coming from his or her mouth. To be able to listen, you need to try to understand the context along with the content of what a person is saying. You need to be curious, to dig into what the person is saying and why. This takes practice; it does not come easily. I am now using affirmations to help me be a better listener.

Good listeners ask questions and then ask follow-up questions. They qualify what is being said. A good listener paraphrases what has been said to ensure that he/she understands, and then asks a follow-up question. A good listener does not just tell or throw out his/her opinion – "Here, this is what I think."

3) Relationship first

Good listening does not mean you have to agree with what the person is saying, but it does mean that you value the person. This past weekend, I had a heavy, but fun, debate with a friend over a popular political issue. I did not agree with what he was saying, but before I sought to refute the point, I focused on trying to truly understand his perspective. By my focusing on what he was saying and showing that I valued him, he was not offended that I disagreed with what he was saying. He actually said that it was fun to have such a discussion. If I had not truly listened, it would have been two people talking into the air. With that type of "listening," the "air" is the only "one" that will see my point of view.

The most effective way to win an argument or communicate an idea is to listen and ask effective questions. Questions are far more powerful than statements. Questions show that the other person has value. By asking questions, you enable or allow the other person to come to your conclusion through his or her own reasoning or awareness. Good listening is one of the strongest ways to show that you care.

Are You Offensive?

A truly offensive person is one who is a poor listener. An offensive person interrupts what you are saying to speak. He or she dominates the conversation, or he/she stays aloof, not engaged. I have spent time with a person who was a poor listener but a great talker. I rarely could complete more than two sentences without being interrupted. I was exhausted after being with the person just a few hours. This person cared not for what I had to say, but just liked to hear himself talk. I have been that offensive person before. Have you?

Parents, do you truly listen to your children and ask questions to help them see why you want them to do something or not do something? Do you listen when they are frustrated, hurt, struggling with social issues, or do you just try to fix the problem or fix them? For teens, listening is more important than talking. Asking open-ended questions is better than stating your opinion!

Husbands and wives, do you really listen to what your spouse is saying, or are you more concerned with hearing yourself talk and airing your opinions?

Bosses, do you truly hear your employees' problems? Salespeople, are you truly listening to your customers' needs, or are you just trying to sell them your product or services?

The most effective and least offensive way to persuade someone to your point of view is through asking a question, not telling him or her what to think or do.

Faith

James 1: 19 – *"Everyone should be quick to listen, slow to speak and slow to become angry."*

Proverbs 4: 1 – *"Listen, my son, to a father's instruction; pay attention and gain understanding."*

Proverbs 8: 1 – *"Does not wisdom call out? Does not understanding raise her voice?"*

It is amazing how talking gets us into trouble. Jesus encouraged us to keep our mouths shut and our ears open. When we are talking, we can't hear what is being said. These passages are very clear that we should listen more. These passages do not just relate to our earthly relationships, but also to our heavenly relationships. Do you just tell God what you want, or do you listen to what He has to say? Is your prayer life a list of "I want," "I need" or "Please help"? Have you ever asked God to help you listen and hear Him? Have you ever said, "God, I am going to be silent in this prayer time and listen for you to speak"? When reading scripture, ask God to help you hear His voice and how His words should apply to your life.

Most of us want to have wisdom and understanding. What does it take to get those? Listening. Remember, if you are talking all the time, you can't hear God when He gives you wisdom and understanding.

Practice being quiet and listening!

I read this _ _ _ _ _ _ _ times this week.

What Do You Give and How Do You Give It?

You have heard that it is more blessed to give than receive. The questions I ask is, "What are you giving?" Depending on what you are giving, you may not be blessed at all, and the receiver may actually be hurt, insulted or cursed.

If what you give is valuable, then you are blessed, and so is the receiver. If what you give is destructive, then both you and the receiver are worse off.

Here are few examples of what I am talking about:

Do you give a smile to someone, or a frown?
Do you give a complaint or a compliment?
Do you encourage others or make disparaging remarks?
Are you characterized by being a negative person or a positive person?
Do you give warm relationships or alienation?
Do you not give at all but just take?

Attitude and Motivation of Giving

Do you give money to others? If so, do you do it with a cheerful heart or out of obligation? If out of obligation, then you will eventually become bitter and resent those to whom you have been giving. If out of joy you give, then you will be excited to see others receive your gift.

Do you give just to make yourself feel better? Do you give to get something back? If so, you will never find giving totally satisfying. It will never be enough. If you give because you care for others, then the gift is satisfying and can be complete.

Do you give your time, and is it done with a cheerful heart?

Do you give your attention to listen, or just keep quiet while the other person talks?

Do you give value to your spouse, children, co-workers, boss, community and country?

I have heard people say about another, "That person does not give at all; they just take." Well, that statement is not completely true. For even a taker gives something back – ingratitude, bitterness, self-centeredness, anger, animosity or fear.

Everyone gives; decide today what you will give.

I try to give away a "Good morning" and smile to at least five people before 9 AM each day. I try to give eye contact at the checkout counter, along with a smile. I work on giving a positive attitude at work and when I come home from work. Be a good listener. That is truly a great gift.

Faith

2 Corinthians 9: 7-8 – *"Each man should give what he has decided in his heart to give, not reluctantly or under compulsion, for God loves a cheerful giver. And God is able to make all grace abound to you, so that in all things at all times, having all that you need, you will abound in every good work."*

Deuteronomy 15: 10 – *"Give generously to him and do so without a grudging heart; then because of this the Lord your God will bless you in all your work and everything you put your hand to."*

If you are struggling with your attitude in terms of giving, ask God to help you change. Know that God will provide for you through His riches and His glorious grace. You can be a cheerful giver in all things. Start small and let the giving naturally grow. Be a giver, not a taker.

I read this _ _ _ _ _ _ _ times this week.

Being Right vs. Building the Right Relationship

This past weekend I took my daughter target shooting and witnessed an interesting scenario that we have reflected on multiple times.

A young man shot a signal flare from a flare gun at the 100-yard, 40-foot-high, dirt backstop. He expected it to hit the dirt and burn for a little while. Instead, the flare rose up and went over the backstop into the woods and caught a dead tree on fire.

Once that happened, the potential for a forest fire became extreme. The young man and his two friends tried to put it out with water but did not have enough, and the 20-foot tree started to burn.

There were two people witnessing this event. One was a person (Person A) who immediately began to chew out the young men (all three) about shooting off the flare and how stupid they were. (Mind you that only one person shot the flare; the other two were helping fight the fire.) Person A threatened to call the sheriff and continually spoke negatively to the young man and his companions. This man offered no help and alienated everyone at the range.

Another person at the range, Person B, saw what happened, was calm, understanding, offered assistance in the form of a gallon of water and a fire extinguisher. He even went to help fight the fire when it flared up again after the 3 young men left.

Person A threatened to call the sheriff if the young men did not repay Person B for the fire extinguisher. Person B required no such repayment, but said he would take a check if mailed.

Person A left, and in a few minutes the 3 young men left also. Unfortunately, about 10 minutes later the fire restarted.

Person B went over the 40-foot-high dirt mound and into the briars to fight the fire. After ten minutes, another bystander joined him. After 20 minutes of working to get the smoldering wood out, they returned, happily chatting, obviously having made a new friendship.

I share this story to ask the question. Which person are you when someone makes a mistake?

Compare the two people and ask yourself how you typically react.

1) Person A was correct in his judgment but had no compassion; he alienated everyone present and provided no solution, just harsh judgments.

2) Person B vocalized no judgment since the judgment was obvious, and nothing more needed to be said. He offered assistance, showed compassion, consoled the offender, and went the extra mile when the perpetrator left – i.e. accepting new responsibility by fighting the fire.

If you are Person A, everyone thought you were obnoxious – correct in your judgments, but obnoxious. The question I pose, "Was this person just an angry person using another's misfortune to vent his anger?"

Person B was compassionate, respected by all and even benefited by making a new friend.

Who are you? Are you a judging, condemning person who offers no solutions, just self-righteous judgments? Or are you a peacemaker, showing compassion, helping others make restitution and building relationships?

Too many of us are the former and pass that judgmental trait on to our kids. Instead, we should be involved helping the poor, the needy, those who bring problems onto themselves. Many can't pull themselves up by the bootstraps, but require compassionate help, instead of self-righteous judgment.

Faith

In many cases a local church has been like Person A, correctly judging sin, but offering no compassion or willingness to help others out of their troubles. In Jesus' day, this Person A group was the Pharisees. They were quick to judge but offered no help to change the situation.

The reason so many people were attracted to Jesus was that he was the perfect model of Person B. He had compassion, and he provided a solution. He cured the sick, he healed the brokenhearted, and he provided a way to be made new. Jesus got involved in people's lives. Jesus encouraged restitution.

John 8: 3-11 – *"The teachers of the law and the Pharisees brought in a woman caught in adultery. They made her stand before the group and said to Jesus, 'Teacher, this woman was caught in the act of adultery. In the Law Moses commanded us to stone such women. Now what do you say?' They were using this question as a trap, in order to have a basis for accusing him.*

But Jesus bent down and started to write on the ground with his finger. When they kept on questioning him, he straightened up and said to them, 'If any one of you is without sin, let him be the first to throw a stone at her.' Again he stooped down and wrote on the ground.

At this, those who heard began to go away one at a time, the older ones first, until only Jesus was left, with the woman still standing there. Jesus straightened up and asked her, 'Woman, where are they? Has no one condemned you?'

'No one, sir,' she said. 'Then neither do I condemn you,' Jesus declared. 'Go now and leave your life of sin.'"

Recently, my family went to the Yakama Indian reservation in Washington State for a week to serve. Our prayer as we went on the mission trip was that we would be Person B – faithfully

82

reflecting Jesus – and not Person A – judging the Yakama for their poverty and offering no true help.

Please pray for the Yakama people. They are a downtrodden people and a culture that desperately needs redeeming. There is much misery in this people's history.

For more information, please go to
www.sacredroadministries.org.

I read this _ _ _ _ _ _ _ times this week.

Building Relationships
with Trust

Have you ever wanted to help someone who is in a predicament, but whatever you tried did not work? Did they even get mad at you?

Have you ever seen a person or organization try to help the downtrodden, but get rejected by those they are trying to help?

Do you wonder why a person will keep receiving bad advice when that advice never works? Do you ever wonder why people vote for a certain candidate over another?

It all comes down to trust.

In building relationships, you must first establish trust with the other party before you can give them truth. They must trust that you have their best interest at heart before they can listen to you.

Too many people try to fix problems by providing the truth before they ever have established trust in a relationship.

For instance, I work with inner-city black kids. In general, they don't trust white people. They have been taught (or have experienced) that white people are prejudiced and want to keep the black person down. So no matter what I tell those kids about how to better themselves through education, proper speech, etc., they will view me as trying to manipulate them.

The Yakama Indians have the same feelings about whites, for in the past, all their experiences were of whites taking advantage of them. Therefore, when someone comes on the reservation to help, the Yakamas' first response is to reject what that person has to offer.

Trying to fix a problem by presenting truth without first establishing trust leads people to feel manipulated, and they become angry.

But if you spend your time first working to establish trust, then the people you are trying to help will know that you care for them and will be willing to listen to what you have to say.

With the inner-city kids, I spend time with them, from going on field trips to working on goal-setting and character-building. I have invested my time throughout the school year with these kids. In essence, I built trust so that they are willing to hear the truth on how they can better themselves, growing out of poverty. For the Yakama, we established trust by first serving them by painting houses and playing with the kids. The Granberry family (www.sacredroadministry.org) actually moved to the reservation 5 years ago. Family members established relationships and trust before they could begin to help those in poverty.

One political party spends more time on presenting truth: "Here's how I can fix this...," while the other party spends time saying, "Trust me. I will take care of you." Who has the momentum right now?

Once trust is established, a person can hear the truth. The natural progression of a relationship built upon this principle is for the relationship to grow deeper in understanding and commitment, even to a point of love. But if you try to persuade with truth before establishing trust, you will make the other party feel manipulated, and the people you are trying to help might become angry with you, no matter how right you are.

Too many times people assume trust exists where it does not. They proceed (in arrogance, lack of consideration or just in ignorance) to present truth. All they do is just offend the other person. (I now realize many times I took this position, assuming trust existed when I was totally ignorant of the other person's perspective. No wonder others were offended.)

The first principle in establishing trust is to love someone regardless of his or her position or circumstances. Loving first establishes trust, which leads to the opportunity to present truth. Truth's natural progression is to receive love back. Spending time with a person and listening to understand and build a relationship shows love.

How does this apply in your daily life outside of helping the downtrodden?

In marriage does your spouse truly trust you when you confront him or her about a marital problem? What is his/her response? That response will generally give you the answer. Do you truly listen and acknowledge what your spouse has said, or do you just argue back? Listening builds the relationship.

How does your teenager respond when you talk to him or her about a problem he/she has? Does he/she listen or argue? Do you listen and establish trust? How much time do you spend with him or her?

If you are a boss, do your people listen to you out of trust or fear? Your actions speak louder than what you say. Do you build trust through relationships, or are you just focused on the next goal?

When you share your faith, is it out of a pure love for another person, or because you feel you are right and they are wrong?

Trust leads to the opportunity to share truth. Truth given in a trusting relationship leads to love.

A book I just read called *A Same Kind of Different As Me*, by Ron Hall and Denver Moore, is a perfect example of the trust-to-truth-to-love dynamic. Ron is an international art dealer in Houston, and Denver was a modern-day slave who grew up in Louisiana on a plantation, was in prison, then homeless. The book shows how they built a relationship, first on trust, then truth, and now they love each other. This incredible true story was published in 2006.

86

Faith

Psalms 13: 5 – *"But I trust in your unfailing love; my heart rejoices in your salvation."*

Psalms 19: 7-8 – *"The law of the LORD is perfect, reviving the soul. The statutes of the LORD are trustworthy, making wise the simple. The precepts of the LORD are right, giving joy to the heart. The commands of the LORD are radiant, giving light to the eyes."*

God's word was given to us to establish a relationship with Him. Most people think God gave His word to be a killjoy, to tell people what not to do. Many think God is all about interjecting Himself to control their life.

But for those who trust God and believe that He truly loves them, His commands are truth-giving joy to the soul, making wise the simple. God demonstrated His love and built trust by sending His son, Jesus, to first establish relationship, then to tell the truth of man's need for a savior. Jesus then demonstrated his love for all men by dying for them. Thus, this trust of His love leads me to believe His truth and love Him.

I read this _ _ _ _ _ _ _ times this week

What You Believe Drives You

Have you ever taken time and really assessed what you believe? Have you written down each area of your life and then written, "Here is what motivates me or drives me in these areas"? I have. Doing this is difficult, but I did it over a period of a time, addressing each area individually. This exercise has changed my life. I encourage you to begin this process.

Life-Ruining Philosophies

Several philosophies that I once believed were actually ruining my life. These values were driving me, causing stress and taking my attention away from other areas.

Here are several beliefs that I had and am working to change:

1) "More is better" – According to the American dream, the bigger the house, the more expensive the car, the happier the person. Even having extra property or taking a fancy vacation is supposed to make a person happier. I had fallen into this lie and was investigating buying, via a mortgage, 100 acres, and also was beginning to think I needed a bigger house.

The reality is the more I own, the more stress I have in taking care of what I own. The more I own, the more my stuff owns me. There is freedom in having less. I have been enjoying that freedom for the past 2 years. I have not bought a new car and have worked hard to get out of debt. Yes, I have done without, but I am free from the bank owning me, and free from more stuff owning me.

2) "My career matters the most" – I have started a business, and the stress is high; the stakes are high, and I have others depending on me to make sales or payroll. Under those circumstances, it is easy to believe that my work is the most important thing in my life. Well, when I assessed my values, I realized that work comes and goes, but my family is the one

88

stable thing in my life besides God. Over the past 6 months, I have had to deny work to meet family needs. I have to continually remind myself that my wife and kids are far more important than a business. I need less of work and more of them.

3) "My purpose in life is to please me" – The temptation was to pursue a life of comfort and ease. Once I came home from work, the temptation was to check out, to disengage, because that is what was pleasing to me. That attitude alienated my family and caused me to be irritated when someone else needed something. In reality, my purpose in life is truly fulfilled when I love God and when I love my neighbor as myself.

4) "You can lead a private life and have private time" – This mind-set is that certain habits, attitudes or practices don't affect others. A person can have certain vices or hidden activities that don't affect others and thus, he/she reasons, are not really harmful. However, no one is truly an island. All that we do affects others. Our attitudes lead to habits, and habits either are positive or negative. Our actions and attitudes either build relationships or harm them. The area this addresses is especially applicable in business, what you see on the Internet and what you watch or read. Garbage in, garbage out. Everything we do affects others, whether it is intangible or tangible.

5) "You can give more than 100%" – I get tired of hearing people say, "Give 110%." That sounds really good, but what does it really mean? Giving 110% means borrowing from tomorrow and spending it today. This attitude implies that you will never have to pay the piper. All we have is one day, a 24-hour time frame in which we have to live a balanced life. I am learning that stressing out over tomorrow, while it is still today, actually robs me of tomorrow. I am learning to work in today and let tomorrow worry about itself. This is very freeing.

Faith

Ephesians 5: 15-21 – *"Be very careful, then, how you live, not as unwise but as wise, making the most of every opportunity, because the days are evil. Therefore do not be foolish, but understand what the Lord's will is. Do not get drunk on wine, which leads to debauchery. Instead, be filled with the Spirit. Speak to one another with psalms, hymns and spiritual songs. Sing and make music in your heart to the Lord, always giving thanks to God the Father for everything, in the name of our Lord Jesus Christ. Submit to one another out of reverence for Christ."*

These verses are great. These verses are a warning and an encouragement in how to live your life.

1) We are to be wise (that is, being intentional and having discernment) in how we live; we are not just to let time slip by.

2) Make the most of every opportunity. This means don't just disengage, but stay involved and be on the lookout (i.e., have awareness) for opportunity to move forward in your life.

3) Do not be foolish. A fool assumes that he/she is wise. A fool assumes that he or she has all the answers. A fool assumes that he/she doesn't have to work at life. A fool checks out of life, and lets life run over him or her. A fool assumes that he/she doesn't need to change anything. God's will is for us to have a relationship with him, praising him, being under his influence and building relationships with others.

4) Submit to one another. This addresses accountability and your private life. Each one of us is accountable to others in our attitudes and actions. Submission requires humility.

Matthew 6: 34 – *"Therefore do not worry about tomorrow, for tomorrow will worry about itself. Each day has enough trouble of its own."*

Enjoy today, for that is all you have. Stressing over tomorrow changes nothing and just robs you of today.
I read this _ _ _ _ _ _ _ times this week.

Perceptions, Perspectives, Judgments and Principles

I am reading Steven Covey's book *The 7 Habits of Highly Effective People.* This book is very powerful read over and over and applied but is a waste of time if read just once for knowledge. Also, my family just returned from a week of mission work on the Yakama Indian reservation in Washington State, and I have several observations based upon this experience and Covey's book:

1) We are quick to judge based upon our perception of the situation.

Our perspective, i.e. the lens through which we look, determines our perceptions. It is easy to judge in this manner.

I learned that my judgments are not always true and that there is always more to the story. For instance, the Native American is stereotyped as lazy and unwilling to work. But that is our perspective, and *we* are defining "work." This reputation initially came about when the US Government Bureau of Indian Affairs tried to force the Sioux Indians to farm in the Dakotas. The attempt was doomed from the beginning. They were trying to farm in an arid environment with no irrigation and at a time when there was also a severe drought. In actuality, the Native American had a very strong work ethic, but it revealed itself differently via hunting, fishing and gathering. The tribe also placed great value on supporting everyone as a whole, with very little individualism.

2) With no personal experience, the judgment is made that our way is always the best way.

This position may come from insecurity, greed or arrogance. You can not determine if your way is the best way until you truly, not superficially, investigate the other ways. There IS truth, and there are best ways, but most people are lazy and are not willing to investigate. When a person does make the effort to investigate alternatives, the investigation is generally from their value perspective, not from principles.

For instance, because the Native American society focused on community versus individualism, capitalism did not take strong root. Many view this attitude of community as inferior to individualism.

3) To truly know someone, spend time with him or her in his or her daily life.

There is truth about the old saying that it is difficult to understand another until you "walk a mile in his/her shoes."

Jesus, even went beyond that. In Roman times, a person could be conscripted to carry a Roman soldier's pack for a mile. Jesus suggested going an extra mile. If you willingly go the second mile, a relationship begins to be built, and barriers to communication and community and prejudices begin to fall.

Most people who are quick to judge are not willing to get involved. It is easier to be an armchair judge than to commit yourself to understanding. You may believe it to be too risky to get involved; it might change your life.

4) As Steven Covey says, "The way we SEE the problem IS the problem."

Most people want a quick-fix, wrap-it-up type of solution, and therefore they view problems from this perspective. In the case of the Native Americans, in addition to the accusation that they are lazy, many white people claim them to be untrustworthy. The truth is that the Native American does not trust a white man. This is understandable when you see their history and see that for every one white person that was trustworthy, ten cheated them. The US Government was the biggest cheater, because it did not abide by its own treaties.

Most people don't take the time or are not willing to find the underlying chronic problem. Chronic problems take time and lots of effort to change or fix. Most people want to deal with the symptomatic problems and provide a quick fix. This approach to chronic problems IS the problem.

Do you approach marriage, parenting or work problems this way? "If the other person would just do this.... my problem would go away." "If my life was better, I would not be angry." "If my kids would behave better...." "I would give if I had more money."

Most chronic problems in relationships are due to a focus on self and not a focus on others. "I am supreme, and therefore all others must adjust to me." The way we SEE the problem IS the problem.

5) Look for principles before you judge with values.

Principles are deep, foundational truths that have universal application and should be our benchmark for judgment, not opinions, perspectives or even values. Covey says that principles are guidelines for human conduct that are proven to have enduring, permanent value. (Values are typically cultural.)

For instance, the principles of courage, discipline, community, love and honesty can be demonstrated in many ways, depending on the culture and the community. In many cases, we take little time to see if these principles actually exist but are being demonstrated in another way than we expect. We apply our cultural value and then make a judgment. We all do this, but the question is, "Are you open to investigating deeper to find the principles?"

For example, a middle-class value is to place emphasis on ownership of things. A value demonstrated in Native American communities is to place value and literal ownership on relationships more than on things. Where a middle-class person will spend money to maintain an item, a Yakama Indian will spend money to build a relationship and neglect the maintenance of the item.

As a result of this cultural difference and value, I had the tendency to judge in thinking, "These people don't care about what they own and are poor stewards." In actuality, the principle that they are demonstrating is "Love your neighbor as yourself." They have limited funds, so they are spending funds where they matter the most, on people, not things. By maintaining my car, my house, and other material possessions, I could actually be guilty of the negative principle of greed, or being self-centered instead of spending time or money building relationships. From a middle-class cultural value, looking from the outside, I was doing the right thing. From a principle standpoint, looking from the inside at my own heart, I was guilty of not doing the right thing, of not loving another.

The applications to these concepts are:

1) Spend your time developing worthwhile principles
2) Be willing to listen to another's viewpoint
3) Be willing to get involved to truly learn. As Covey says, "Admission of ignorance is the first step in our education."
4) Examine yourself. Are you living by principles or by convenient cultural values that make pleasing yourself as the true principle?

Faith

Matthew 19: 19 – *"Love your neighbor as yourself."*

In this Jesus was speaking to Jews about Jews, so they all shared the same cultural values and Biblical principles. If your neighbor is not a Jew, then he/she may want to be loved in a different cultural way, not your way; thus the story of the Good Samaritan.

I have heard that the modern translation would be, "Love your neighbor as they would want you to love them."

Are you loving your kids or spouse the way they want you to love them, or are you doing it your way, the convenient way? Have you taken time to actually find out how your spouse or kids would like you to love them? Do you even care?

What about your neighbor? Have you actually walked over and spent more than two minutes going beyond talking about the weather? Do you know what is going on in his life, his hurts, pains, problems or celebrations?

What about your customers? Do you take time to learn their industry, their problems, or are you just wanting to make a quick sale? Do you really care about customer service and meeting customers' needs, or do you just want them to go away when they come with a complaint? The list could go on.

Do you view others as a means to get what you want? I suggest you look at the underlying principle to that perspective.

To learn principles that are life-changing, you must study. Reading the Bible just once does not get it, just as reading your Biology book only once wouldn't teach all of Biology. You don't truly learn it, so you can't apply it. Just going to church on Sunday with no reading or self-assessment during the week gives you a good warm feeling, but no life-changing experience.

Examine yourself: Are you going to church for self, to give you a good feeling? If so, your "act" of worship looks good (cultural value), but your principle is rotten, for you are going not to worship or to benefit others, but just for yourself.

Principles supersede perceptions.

I read this _ _ _ _ _ _ _ times this week

Being a Good Father

On a Father's Day I was able to spend the weekend with my 11-year-old daughter. We went to the mountains. We camped, hiked, played, kayaked and just "hung out." What a great time I had! Being a Dad is great if you have a good relationship with your children.

Here are several behaviors that I have focused on as a Dad to create a good relationship with my children. Adapt them to your situation.

1) Listening, especially for girls, is more important than talking. Be intrigued with what your children say, even if it is just imaginative. Ask questions about what they are telling you. If you have not learned to listen to your children when they are young, they won't listen to you when they are older...teenagers.

2) Let your children tell you about their day. Don't try to fix any problems; just let them talk it out. Ask questions, but don't fix. Many times they just need to know that you are interested in their life.

3) Play games with your kids, young or older. Find a game that interests them, even if you have to learn a new one. Go to the store with your child and pick a game. Focus on playing the game and having a good time, not always on winning. My kids are competitive and so am I, but I show them what good sportsmanship is, win or lose. My teenager is into throwing the Frisbee, so we go outside and throw after work. We talk as we throw. This gives her the opportunity to download and for me to relax after work.

4) Be patient with your children if they are learning to do something you love. Don't push them too hard. I took my youngest to the river to learn to kayak, which is my favorite sport. She was intimidated with even the small whitewater on the river. It was nothing to me, but to her, it was huge. Observing her intimidation, I went at her pace. She did great,

but one day was enough. The next day we played in the lake. The focus on the trip and the events was relationship-building, not learning to kayak. With that focus, we both had a great time.

5) Be firm in instruction, get their attention and have them answer with a "Yes sir" or "No sir." Having your children verbally respond in that manner tells their brain that they are going to obey, and they do. We camped next to a woman who just yelled at her kids the whole weekend. The kids did not begin to obey until she yelled, so she yelled all the time. Yelling just belittles the children and makes the adult look really stupid, as my daughter commented. The only reason the woman resorted to yelling is that she would repeat herself 4-5 times, and then yell. If she required her children to obey the first time, as we observed the Dad required, she would not have to yell. Your kids actually appreciate having to obey the first time. Requiring this type of obedience cuts the guessing game of how many times the parents have to ask before they really get serious. Requiring this type of obedience also reduces household stress.

6) Tell your kids that you love them often and in many different ways. One of those ways may be "no." We say "no" many times to our children. This happens when they want to do something that will take away from family time or add another activity to an already busy schedule. Many families are falling apart because parents aren't saying "no" but instead are catering to every activity or whim for which a child asks. Saying "no" sets boundaries. Children want boundaries. If you set and enforce boundaries at a young age, when they are older, they will expect boundaries as a teenager and will be less likely to challenge your authority. If you have little authority now, do you really expect to have more authority when they are teenagers?

7) Date your kids – whether girls or boys, parents should spend special time with each child at least once a month. In our family, I take one child out to dinner, or do something fun with one while my wife takes the other. The next month we swap up. If you and your spouse want to spend time with a child, that's

great, but make sure you are focusing the day or evening on building a relationship with your child. My daughters know how to be properly treated by a boy, because I am already showing them how a boy should act.

Faith

In 1 Samuel 2, Eli and his two sons were priests for Israel before King David came along. Eli was an indulgent father and did not discipline his two sons. As they continued in their wickedness, Eli did nothing to stop them. In 1 Samuel 2, there is a prophecy against Eli and his two sons. Because Eli did nothing to stop their wickedness, God also held Eli accountable for their wickedness. Eli was not faithful in the greatest area of responsibility that God had given him, being a father.

Colossians 3: 21 – *"Fathers, do not embitter your children, or they will become discouraged."*

How you talk to your children and how you discipline your children can either build strong bonds or create an embittered child. If you discipline in anger, your children will remember it. If you talk in condescending tones or are always negative, they will remember. If you try to relive your life through your kids, they will resent it. Rebellion in a teenager may actually stem from how they were treated as a child.

Many parents ask, "What happened to the youth of today?" In many cases, what actually should be asked is, "What happened to concerned, involved, disciplined parents?"

A great book on raising a child from the inside out is *Shepherding Your Child's Heart* by Tedd Tripp.

Start being a great Dad today!

I read this _ _ _ _ _ _ _ times this week

Leaving a Legacy

As a parent, what is one of the greatest legacies you can leave to your children? Good character. What is good character? In this book, good character covers two areas in particular: 1) how you treat and deal with others and 2) how you treat and deal with yourself.

How You Treat Others

The Golden Rule, "Do unto others as you would have them do unto you," is a universal rule. Sociologists report that the principle of the golden rule is found in every society. Every people group teaches the same character values: honor others; treat others are you would like to be treated.

If we were to ask that question in another way – "How does this person want to be treated?" – it might cause us to re-assess what we say or what we do. In teaching our children, remember, "More is caught than taught." Our actions speak louder than our words. One of the key attitudes that determines how we treat others is our pride. Our pride will determine the real legacy we leave, whether we leave a legacy of broken relationships or strong, heartwarming, secure relationships.

How You Treat and Deal with Yourself

Several questions will help you determine what type of character you have and are building in your children, peers or employees:

1) Do you tell yourself you deserve something, especially over another person?

2) Do you justify to yourself your actions or lack of actions either by saying, "I deserve it" or "It is someone else's fault or responsibility"?

3) Are you quick to point the finger at someone else, but rarely

admit your guilt?

4) Do you let yourself off the hook regularly, but are intolerant of someone else?

5) Do you say, "I'll change when he or she first initiates change or apologizes first"?

6) Do you justify your laziness or inactivity in work, marriage, family or other relationships?

7) Do you tell yourself, "I'm just too tired to help with ...."?

These issues generally deal with pride. The definition of pride is "a high or inordinate opinion of one's own dignity, importance, merit or superiority, whether as cherished in the mind or as displayed in bearing, conduct, etc."

When you or I have these thoughts, they lead to actions. My actions are then modeled by my children. Is this what I want to leave for my kids?

Pride is the enemy of character and all good relationships. If you are going to practice the Golden Rule, pride will have to go. To get rid of pride, you need to replace pride with something else. I suggest another meaning for the word pride, an acronym I learned from Lt. Clebe McClary (a silver- and bronze-star Vietnam vet who is a leadership and motivational speaker at www.clebemcclary.com).

PRIDE:
Personal Responsibility In Daily Effort

Personal responsibility asks or takes action in many ways:

1) When there is an offense or argument between you and another, personal responsibility takes the initiative by asking, "What can I do to remedy or bring healing to this situation?"

It does not take into account who really is at fault. PRIDE is others-focused.

2) This type of PRIDE initiates action in relationships, especially in marriage or family. It asks, "What have I done today to demonstrate my love for my spouse or kids?" It does not expect to be served.

3) This PRIDE is grateful and expresses thankfulness on a regular basis.

4) This PRIDE does not blame others when things go wrong. It takes personal responsibility to make things better.

5) This type of PRIDE remembers that a person is not an island and that relationships are more important than things or work.

6) PRIDE does not wait for something to happen but creates the moment.

7) This PRIDE constantly helps the downtrodden. It gives at church, to a neighbor and at the office. It is not greedy, nor is it overly self-indulgent.

8) This PRIDE keeps commitments, even when it hurts. It stays put, even in the toughest of times.

9) This PRIDE keeps its priorities, no matter who has to be told "no," even when it means saying "no" to the boss.

10) This PRIDE does not make excuses, but asks for forgiveness, even from his/her children.

Are you struggling in your marriage, in raising your kids, at work or in other relationships? Are you dissatisfied with your life right now? Maybe what is causing the problem is false pride, an inappropriate focus on yourself or what you want and what you are not getting. Replace false pride with true PRIDE, which leads to humility, re-union, wholeness, and satisfaction in life.

What will be your legacy?

Faith

Psalms 10: 4 – *"In his pride the wicked does not seek him; in all his thoughts there is no room for God."*

Psalms 31: 18 – *"Let their lying lips be silenced, for with pride and contempt they speak arrogantly against the righteous."*

Proverbs 11: 2 – *"When pride comes, then comes disgrace, but with humility comes wisdom."*

Proverbs 13: 10 – *"Pride only breeds quarrels, but wisdom is found in those who take advice."*

Proverbs 16: 18 – *"Pride goes before destruction and a haughty spirit before a fall."*

Proverbs 29: 23 – *"A man's pride brings him low, but a man of lowly spirit gains honor."*

Is there a relationship that is broken that needs mending, but pride is keeping you from doing it? Is there someone from whom you need to ask forgiveness, but pride is keeping your from doing it? Is there some service or special thing that your spouse asks of you, but pride keeps you from doing it? Are you spending time at work because of pride about your work, when you should be home with your family? Does pride cause you to have the wrong focus of your time, money or relationships? Pride leads to destruction, but in humility and repentance, there are forgiveness and grace. Which do you want?

Because pride is such an evil thing that is not easily cast aside, ask God to help you change. Seek true wisdom in a relationship with your creator.

I read this _ _ _ _ _ _ times this week.

Dignity, Respect, Humility
vs. Pride

In the last segment, I talked about leaving a legacy and the effect pride has on all relationships, especially with our children.

Another way to look at pride and its effects on our relationships is to ask the question, "Did my actions toward a certain person treat him or her with dignity and respect?" That is a very hard question, because you may think that person deserved what you said or did. Unfortunately, you may think certain people do not deserve respect and have no dignity. This mindset enables you to justify your actions, whether in parenting, marriage, work or driving.

What is interesting is that the greater our pride, the easier it is to justify not treating another person with dignity and respect. Some examples that have shown up in my life are in parenting, in marriage or even in my driving habits. Have you run any red lights lately?

Parenting

In parenting, I was more interested in proving that I was right and that my children were wrong than in helping them to correct their attitude or poor behavior. In proving that I was right, I did not treat the child with dignity or respect. In doing so, I hurt the relationship and lowered the trust factor with my daughter. I have learned that it takes a lot of good, respectful actions to make up for one disrespectful action.

In disciplining children, it is many times easier to focus on the punishment and making them "pay" than to focus on the desired outcome of the discipline. With pride driving our minds, it is easier and more expedient to lash out in anger than to stop, think and treat the other person with respect and dignity. In raising our children, our goal should be to bring them up so that they can function in society, showing others respect and treating others with dignity.

Marriage

In marital conflict, pride shows up by a spouse yelling at the other, giving the cold shoulder or just saying, "I'll do my thing while she does hers." Pride likes to show itself in the heat of the moment, when we can so easily justify to ourselves why we don't need to treat the person with dignity and respect.

Work

At work, do you treat your peers or subordinates with an attitude of pride or of humility? Are your actions communicating that that employee is a person and deserves respect? Does your pay scale treat people with dignity, or do you take advantage of them because you can? Do your employees know you care, or do they know you could care less?

Driving

In my driving, I have justified running a red light because my plans were too important to wait. I did not think about the other drivers and how I could endanger or even kill someone.

At times, I do run across a person whose behavior is so repulsive that I don't want to treat him or her with dignity and respect. But I have learned that if I stop treating that person with dignity and respect, I begin the path to become like him or her.

Taking Personal Inventory

This list below was given to me, and I thought it was worth republishing. Ask yourself which way you tend to lean – pride or humility? Ask your wife, husband, child or friend to rate their top three strengths and weaknesses in the following list.

Many people think that being humble is a weakness or is lowering yourself. I like these three definitions of humility: a) not proud or arrogant; modest; b) meek, which is defined as controlled strength; c) courteously respectful.

A humble person is in control of himself or herself. He/she doesn't always have to be right or always be in the limelight, nor must he/she always have life be about him or her. A humble person is others-focused.

Attitude of Pride	vs.	Attitude of Humility
Poor listener		Listens attentively and works on listening skills
Rarely affirms others		Affirms often
Has little patience		Bears with others, has patience
Holds grudges		Forgives and moves on
Ignores people he/she dislikes		Respects all
Needs to win conflicts		Loves and seeks to understand others
Judges quickly		Forgives quickly
Gossips, blame-shifts		Controls tongue
Compares self with others		Honors others
Minimizes or denies weaknesses		Admits weaknesses
"I can do all things"		"How can I help?"
"What's in it for me?"		Gives selflessly

Faith

Genesis 3: 1-5 – *"Now the serpent was more crafty than any of the wild animals the LORD God had made. He said to the woman, 'Did God really say, "You must not eat from any tree in the garden?"' The woman said to the serpent, 'We may eat fruit from the trees in the garden, but God did say, "You must not eat fruit from the tree that is in the middle of the garden, and you must not touch it, or you will die."' 'You will not surely die,' the serpent said to the woman. 'For God knows that when you eat of it your eyes will be opened, and you will be like God, knowing good and evil.'"*

This is the beginning of pride. Pride is elevating yourself above another. Adam and Eve wanted to be like or as God. It is the original sin from which all other sins are derived.

Proverbs 22: 4 – *"Humility and the fear of the LORD bring wealth and honor and life."*

Matthew 5: 5 – *"Blessed are the meek [controlled strength] for they shall inherit the earth."*

This is not a blessing for a wimpy person, but for one who knows his/her strength and controls it and uses it properly. This is a person who submits to God's authority in life.

I read this _ _ _ _ _ _ times this week.

Where is Your Heart?

I am reading a book called *Lost in the Middle* by Paul David Tripp, and this question is raised several times: "Where is your heart?" It has caused me to re-examine much of what I do and why I do it.

Where our heart is, there also is our treasure.

Our motivations are derived from the things that we treasure or on which we place great value. Have you ever asked yourself, "What motivates me in my: work, marriage, friendships, parenting, finances, health or spiritual areas of my life?"

We tend not to ask such questions but just roll along, pursuing those things we treasure without looking at their long-term value. Or if we do identify that we need to change in an area, do we mitigate our guilt or feelings of discomfort by equating acknowledgment of the problem to actual change? Do we say, "There, I admit I have a problem. OK, that's solved."?

Asking the Tough Questions of Ourselves

These questions need to be asked, because what we treasure can either lead to blessing or lead to pain, misery or loneliness.

There are typically two types of attitudes that characterize each area of a person's life: 1) life is about me and making me happy, or 2) life is about others and my relationship to them.

Life Questions

Here are some examples of how these attitudes are played out:

1) Finances – Do you complain about not having enough, or do you look for ways to benefit others with what you have? It is interesting to note that the middle class and poor give far more

in proportion to their income than do the wealthy. The more we have, the more we tend to protect it.

Do you spend everything you have and get yourself into debt because you can't wait and have to have something now?

2) Family – Do you come home from work and expect others to serve you or not bother you? Or do you come home and are concerned how your spouse's or children's day went and then talk with them? Do you primarily encourage your spouse and kids, or are you critical?

3) Leisure – Do you view leisure as an end in itself – you need leisure, for it is your right? Or do you view leisure as a way to rejuvenate yourself so you can continue to fulfill your responsibilities?

4) Relationships – Do you look at others in view of what they can do for you? Or do you look at relationships as give and take – you support them; they support you? Do you avoid doing what you know you should do, because it makes you uncomfortable? Do you know you need to change an attitude or habit but don't because it requires effort? Do you justify your actions by saying, "Well, that's just the way I am."?

5) Health – Do your eating habits reflect that you are concerned about your health? Do you exercise? Typically, if we are only concerned about ourselves, we are not concerned about eating healthfully or exercising.

Has exercising, health, cosmetics, etc. become ends in themselves to the point that you are so concerned about how you look that your looks take priority over other areas or people?

6) Career – Are you struggling in your career because you are not willing to put forth the effort or take the necessary risk? Do you need to change an attitude or behavior at work? Do you need to learn something new or get out of your comfort zone? Are you working to win or working to prevent a loss? Winning is looking forward; preventing a loss is looking behind you.

7) Spiritual and ethical – Are there attitudes that you need to change? Do you have any absolutes, or is everything relative to you? Do you attend church only when it is convenient? Do you lead your family in this area or leave it up to your spouse? Do you practice what you preach in front of your kids, your spouse or co-workers? Is your word reliable? Can people count on you?

If any of these areas of your life is primarily focused on making *you* happy, be careful; you are headed for disappointment or a shipwreck.

Faith

Matthew 6: 19-21 – *"Do not store up for yourselves treasures on earth, where moth and rust destroy, and where thieves break in and steal. But store up for yourselves treasures in heaven, where moth and rust do not destroy, and where thieves do not break in and steal. For where your treasure is, there your heart will be also."*

Matthew 6: 25-34 – *"Therefore I tell you, do not worry about your life, what you will eat or drink; or about your body, what you will wear. Is not life more important than food, and the body more important than clothes? Look at the birds of the air; they do not sow or reap or store away in barns, and yet your heavenly Father feeds them. Are you not much more valuable than they? Who of you by worrying can add a single hour to his life?*

And why do you worry about clothes? See how the lilies of the field grow. They do not labor or spin. Yet I tell you that not even Solomon in all his splendor was dressed like one of these. If that is how God clothes the grass of the field, which is here today and tomorrow is thrown into the fire, will he not much more clothe you, O you of little faith? So do not worry, saying, 'What shall we eat?' or 'What shall we drink?' or 'What shall we wear?' For the pagans run after all these things, and your heavenly Father knows that you need them. But seek first his kingdom and his righteousness, and all these things will be given to you as well. Therefore do not worry about tomorrow, for tomorrow will worry about itself. Each day has enough trouble of its own."

Jesus encourages and instructs us to set our hearts on things above and to be focused on his kingdom and righteousness. This is the opposite of focusing on self.

I read this _ _ _ _ _ _ _ times this week.

Deceiving Yourself?

As I write these weekly lessons, I have to ask myself, "Do I merely write about these issues, or do I really practice what I am writing about?"

I recently spent a day reviewing the questions that I had posed in the previous chapter. I was trying to apply these truths in my own life.

Challenged with the Truth

Often when we are faced with information about our habits, moral issues or attitudes, we realize we are confronted with truths that we are not applying. Many times, uncomfortable truths challenge us to change. We all must realize that it is easy to acknowledge that information is something of value, but then fail to make any real change. Are you characterized by agreeing with someone, "Yeah, that's right; I believe that," but then not working to apply it to your own life? Do you yell, "Preach it, brother!" but then don't apply what is being preached?

Lying to Yourself

It is easy to acknowledge some information as truth and to chart the correct course for others, but it is very difficult for us to apply it to our own lives. The practice of hearing and then acknowledging beneficial or challenging information, but not applying or "doing" it, leads to an attitudinal trap. You begin to tell yourself that you believe, and that is enough.

There is another type of person who, when presented with truth, feels guilty and then changes his or her behavior for a short time. This short time of behavior change eliminates the guilt. He/she thinks, "There, I have conquered that problem." The fallacy in that type of behavior is that the root attitude has not changed. Without the attitude changing, there is never lasting behavior change.

There are many areas of a person's life that need to be constantly addressed. Big changes may be needed or just little adjustments in an area in which you are weak or need to have your attitude fine-tuned.

Excuses

The problem is that if we don't continually monitor our lives and check to see if we are drifting, we then begin to tell ourselves little lies to avoid change or guilt. Here are a few:

1) That area is really not important in life or my relationships.

2) That's not comfortable to me to do, so I don't have to do it. It is OK for ME to neglect that area. I'm too busy.

3) It's not my fault; my personality is that way. I just like to work on the little details and not see the big picture. Or, I am a big picture person; I don't need to manage the details.

4) I conquered that issue two years ago. It doesn't matter now.

5) Well, he or she will just have to get over it. I am not going to change.

The list could go on forever. We come up with so many reasons to justify our behavior or self-centered attitudes.

Slippery Slope

A person who acknowledges truth or a moral value but then does not work to implement it is on shaky ground. (Many times you can't work on the issue without outside help, so seek help if you need it.) Several things can happen to a person who refuses to change. Every time he/she sees or hears that truth in practice and doesn't respond with repentance and effort:

1) His/her heart becomes a little more calloused or insulated to hearing the truth the next time.

114

2) He/she continues to downgrade the priority or value of the truth. The person starts saying that the truth is "relative" or "OK for you, but not for me."

3) He/she finally becomes deceived and justifies his/her actions, even when it is obvious to everyone that the actions are wrong. If opposed, the person might become angry and blame others.

Being deceived, we will justify our actions to no end. We will blame others, or our circumstances, and even blame the weather.

Working to Change

Learning a truth and applying that truth is good **PRIDE**, **P**ersonal **R**esponsibility **I**n **D**aily **E**ffort. You may need to seek help in applying it.

If there is an area that you see where you are weak and you know you need to change, here are a few suggestions:

1) Write down the specific points of your weakness and what attitude you think causes them. Then write down the attitude and action you want to apply or adopt. Post the positive attitude and habit where you can read it once a day.

2) Develop a list of actions you will take to address these issues. Write these down, including how you will work on your new attitude. You must focus on attitude, for actions are not lasting until attitude is changed.

3) Be accountable to someone else. Share your list of actions, new attitude and goal for a new habit with someone who will help and encourage you through this process.

4) Get counseling if needed. Seek the counsel of someone who has this part of his or her life under control.

Faith

James 1: 22-26 – *"My dear brothers, take note of this: Everyone should be quick to listen, slow to speak and slow to become angry, for man's anger does not bring about the righteous life that God desires. Therefore, get rid of all moral filth and the evil that is so prevalent and humbly accept the word planted in you, which can save you.*

Do not merely listen to the word, and so deceive yourselves. Do what it says. Anyone who listens to the word but does not do what it says is like a man who looks at his face in a mirror and, after looking at himself, goes away and immediately forgets what he looks like. But the man who looks intently into the perfect law that gives freedom, and continues to do this, not forgetting what he has heard, but doing it, he will be blessed in what he does.

If anyone considers himself religious and yet does not keep a tight rein on his tongue, he deceives himself, and his religion is worthless."

The Bible tells us there are three steps to change:

1) Repenting by being sorry and seeking forgiveness

2) Believing that by and through God's grace you are forgiven

3) Working out this new attitude and behavior.

True and lasting change requires all three. It is easy to try to do only two, but true change only comes with all three. Decide to change today!

I read this _ _ _ _ _ _ times this week.

Going from Thinking to Doing

I had a short conversation with a friend today. He is facing some challenging circumstances that will require him to get out of his comfort zone, possibly change an attitude and set new goals.

His comments and attitude were quite natural, but just the opposite of what he needed. He was looking back, fearing change and looking for someone or something to bail him out.

When we face new challenges, hardships or other situations, there is a tendency to get bogged down with several attitudes or behaviors. We "know" intellectually what to do, but our attitudes and habits have never adopted the right practices, so we really don't know at all.

Facing Difficulties – Two Choices

When you are facing difficulties or other challenges, do you:

1) Listen to yourself or specifically talk to yourself? We tend to listen to all our fears, every negative possibility that could possibly happen. We listen to our pain or fear and tend to protect ourselves in our thoughts and attitudes. To overcome obstacles and change attitudes, we don't need to listen to ourselves; we need to specifically talk to ourselves. We need to put the positive, proactive, "can do" thoughts in our mind. We need to focus on what we want to accomplish and make THAT the dominant thought of our mind. Take control of your mind! Affirmations are invaluable in taking control of your mind.

2) Do you look back and yearn or look forward and plan? Most, when faced with a potential loss, look at the past or look at what others have and covet. Life Leaders look to the future and plan. A plan, even when it has to be changed, is better than winging it

every time. Is your plan written down? Have you discussed your plan with others? Have you identified the obstacles you will face and how to overcome them?

3) How you talk to others – Do you speak in terms of wishes or regrets? Do you speak negatively of another? All this is in the past. Nothing changes in the past. Your speech should be filled with positive statements of what you are planning for the future, not on all the negative stuff that has happened or is even happening!

4) Do you sit down and pout, or do you assume responsibility to make changes? Do you ask for others to help you, or do you seek help from others, such as, "Help me, for I can't or won't help myself?" Are you seeking others to bail you out, when you need to take responsibility?

5) Do you worry? When we worry, we feel like we are "doing" something, but in reality we are doing nothing. Worrying not only does nothing but actually takes away from what could be done. If you are worrying, then you are not working on a solution. If you are worrying about tomorrow, you are borrowing from what could be done today. If you are worrying about what happened in the past, you are stealing from today and tomorrow. Worrying steals time away from productive thinking, hurts our health and de-motivates us.

Walking the Talk

The summary of all this is that many talk and say, "I know all that," but few actually put it into practice. Those who claim to "know all that," but don't do it, really just see the truth from afar. It is not theirs. They have never crossed the river to experience it. Are you sitting on one side of the river, hoping someone might bring you a boat? Are you waiting for someone to deliver you? Take action. Nothing changes until YOU change!

We live in America. There is no other country in the world where, if you don't like your circumstances, you can work to change them. We have all the freedom in the world, but few are really willing to take it advantage of our freedom.

Faith

Philippians 3: 12-14 – *"Not that I have already obtained all this, or have already been made perfect, but I press on to take hold of that for which Christ Jesus took hold of me. Brothers, I do not consider myself yet to have taken hold of it. But one thing I do: Forgetting what is behind and straining toward what is ahead, I press on toward the goal to win the prize for which God has called me heavenward in Christ Jesus."*

When I struggle with an attitude or behavior, I find a Bible verse that addresses the issue. I write it down on a 3x5 card and place it on my car dashboard. I typically will read that verse between 5-10 times per week until my attitude begins to change.

Are you pressing on or just sitting down?

I read this _ _ _ _ _ _ _ times this week.

Perseverance –
Keep Going; Don't Quit

Have you ever felt like it is not worth going on – not worth giving the effort on a particular project, goal or relationship? I have. I am right in the middle of a tough time getting a business launched. There are many days I just want to throw in the towel and quit.

One of the questions I ask myself is, "Have I conditioned myself to give up or to stick it out when times are tough? Am I teaching my children to give in and give up or to stick it out?"

Americans Can Have Too Many Choices

As Americans, we are used to instant or near-term gratification. We have so many choices that if the going gets tough, we can just choose another path. In many ways, this environment of never-ending choices teaches us and conditions us not to have commitment.

Our lives are so relatively easy compared to the rest of the world that if we don't like the circumstances, we can change them. This freedom is both positive and negative. On the positive side, look at what Americans have achieved! On the negative side, look at the divorce rate. Americans have the highest divorce rate in the world – 5 divorces per 1,000 people! Look at the diet fads; instead of staying committed to a healthy lifestyle, we want a quick fix. Ever bought something you "just *had* to have" on a credit card? Debt has skyrocketed because of impatience.

The Impatient Age

Because we are in an environment of quick fixes and instant gratification, we have become highly impatient. Americans in general don't go for the long haul. We focus on self and complain that the computer is too slow. We run red lights because we can't wait 2-3 minutes for the next green light. We end relationships because it is the other person's fault, not ours. We want instant victory in a war.

With this mindset, today's Americans would not have liberated this country from England. We would have given up after the debacle of losing New York to the British in 1776. George Washington and his Continental Army did not quit. They withdrew and reorganized to win victories throughout New England the following year.

Steps to Keep Going

Here are a few suggestions that I use to keep going when the going gets tough. I hope they encourage you to do the same.

1) Focus on the goal and all its benefits. Write these down. Post them in a prominent place and read them regularly. I keep the words "Achievement," "Creativity," "Freedom" and "Accomplishment" posted on my white board at work.

2) Get someone else's perspective on your issue. Your perspective may be one-sided, warped, narrow-minded or narcissistic.

3) Get an accountability and encouragement partner or a group – people with whom you can share your struggles. Ask them to pray for you. I know several people who send out a prayer request/update email every 4-6 weeks.

4) Take a step back – take a rest, recuperate, recharge your batteries. If it is a relationship in turmoil, temporary separation may be needed.

5) Use affirmations to help you persevere and be committed. For instance, "I am a committed person. I see things to their completion." "I am committed to this marriage and will work through our problems." "I am a healthy person." "I am tough and stick it out."

6) Read books/stories of how others persevered under extreme difficulties. Listen to positive tapes or CDs.

7) Exercise – it clears the mind and gives you energy.

8) Just keep plodding – don't quit. Zig Ziglar tells a story that life is like a deep well. You begin pumping the hand pump, and you don't know exactly when the water will come out. It may come in the next pump, or it may come in another 20 pumps. If you quit, you will have wasted a lot of energy for no reward. The hardest part of the mountain climb, many times, is the last 10%.

9) When you fall down, get up. When you are thrown from the horse, get back on. It may be just that simple.

In life, to achieve your goal, it takes more than effort; it takes commitment.

122

Faith

2 Corinthians 4: 8-10 — *"We are hard pressed on every side, but not crushed; perplexed, but not in despair; persecuted, but not abandoned; struck down, but not destroyed. We always carry around in our body the death of Jesus, so that the life of Jesus may also be revealed in our body. For we who are alive are always being given over to death for Jesus' sake, so that his life may be revealed in our mortal body."*

Paul was willing to go through hard times — shipwrecks, beatings, sleepless nights, hunger, persecutions and even being stoned — all for the sake of his commitment to Christ. His goal was making Christ known. His hope was in heaven, not on earth.

I read this _ _ _ _ _ _ _ times this week.

Life Directions:
Where Are You Looking?

There are three perspectives or directions from which we can look at our life: the past, the present and the future. Depending on what age you are and your circumstances, you may be looking one way more than the others. The direction you are looking also depends upon what area of your life you are examining: health, finances, relationships, mental, career or spiritual.

Life is much like a farm, and we are the farmers. We have different fields according to each area of our life. How those fields turn out depends on how much time we spent watering, cultivating and weeding the field. How straight our rows are and what we have planted depends on our values, goals, discipline, habits, and on our constantly checking our progress toward our goals.

The book *Lost in the Middle* by Paul Tripp deals with the issues people face in mid-life. When you hit mid-life, whatever time that is for you, you start looking back to see what you have planted and cultivated and to see what is harvested. At this stage in life, adults spend a good bit of time looking back at the life they have lived. As Tripp states, looking back can be disorienting and uncomfortable. You may look and see just weeds or very crooked rows. You may look back and see a field unplanted, overrun with weeds, covered with bushes and rocks or even ruined.

What many in life don't realize is that we are all planting, and we will harvest what we plant. In mid-life you begin to see your harvest. To many, the harvest is painful, unfulfilling or not turning out the way they had expected. The temptation is to then look over the fences and see someone else's field and feel jealousy, envy or regret. The temptation is to see yourself as a victim and tell yourself, "I deserve better. This is not what I had planned." Unfortunately, this type of thinking can lead to ruined relationships, divorce, adultery, going into more debt, getting mad at God or other unwise decision-making.

For those in mid-life who are reaping the harvest, your attitude will determine what you do with the rest of your life. If you see yourself as a victim of circumstances, you will keep making bad decisions and can even make your life more miserable at a future harvest time through divorce, bad health, bankruptcy or loss of job. If you see that your planting was and is under your control, you can begin to weed the fields or begin planting all over again, setting wholesome goals that benefit everyone. Yes, sometimes it is too late to start over; the field is ruined and the soil no longer productive. In this case, repent over your past, and then look for new fields to sow and cultivate with the proper goals, attitudes and relationships. It is never too late to start new.

For those of you in your early stages of life, I encourage you to examine what you are planting, where you are planting and how you are watering. Mid-life regret is a very painful thing. Are you living in the here and now, not considering what you are planting, where you are planting and how straight your rows are? Are you the farmer who is more concerned about your comfort, immediate feelings and gratifying yourself now than about working hard, planting straight rows and looking to the future? Be careful; you may be sowing some terrible weeds or leaving a field to *whatever happens*. Some soils, mistreated, can never be re-cultivated. Know that planting straight rows can be very hard and can take lots of correction, but they are well worth the effort and discipline, with no regrets.

"The unexamined life is not worth living." – Socrates

Faith

Proverbs 2: 1-11 – *"My son, if you accept my words and store up my commands within you, turning your ear to wisdom and applying your heart to understanding, and if you call out for insight and cry aloud for understanding, and if you look for it as for silver and search for it as for hidden treasure, then you will understand the fear of the LORD and find the knowledge of God. For the LORD gives wisdom, and from his mouth come knowledge and understanding. He holds victory in store for the upright; he is a shield to those whose walk is blameless, for he guards the course of the just and protects the way of his faithful ones. Then you will understand what is right and just and fair, every good path. For wisdom will enter your heart and knowledge will be pleasant to your soul.*

Discretion will protect you, and understanding will guard you."

Proverbs 6: 6-11 – *"Go to the ant, you sluggard; consider its ways and be wise! It has no commander, no overseer or ruler, yet it stores its provisions in summer and gathers its food at harvest. How long will you lie there, you sluggard? When will you get up from your sleep? A little sleep, a little slumber, a little folding of the hands to rest, and poverty will come on you like a bandit and scarcity like an armed man."*

Are you being wise, consciously making the right choices? Are you seeking God and his wisdom? Are you setting goals in your own strength? Are you putting off doing something that you know you should do, similar to the sluggard? Where are your heart's desires – on the temporal, which is the here and now, or on the eternal? What harvest will you reap? Will it be full of regret and pain or full of joy and satisfaction? It is never too late to seek God, His wisdom, His forgiveness, His healing and His salvation. All you have to do is ask.

I read this _ _ _ _ _ _ _ times this week.

Life Directions, Part 2 – The Conscientious Farmer

In the last section, I talked about the direction which you are looking: backward, forward or just down. This time, I want to address looking forward – the actual farming process. As I mentioned, life can be compared to a farm, and each area is a unique field: finances, career, mental, spiritual, social, physical and family. What you do in each field determines what you will harvest. As the old proverb goes, "Everyone will reap what he or she sows."

How to Sow and Cultivate for the Harvest

There are several things to consider when tending your fields:

1) Have I chosen a good field and fertile soil? Is what I am planning to build in this area of my life worthwhile, wholesome, stable, long-lasting and fertile, or is it rocky, unfertile, shallow or too soggy? Is this plan culture-driven or principles-driven? Have I even thought about it? In other words, will it have lasting value or harm? Too many times, we just pick any field and start planting before we have assessed if it is truly the best field.

2) How are you plowing? If you have ever watched a farmer plow a field, you've seen that the first two to three rows are the most important ones. These rows set the course that the farmer will follow for the rest of the plowing. Also, if you are using a mule instead of a tractor, it is really difficult, meaning that your life circumstances are not as easy or as favorable as someone else's. A mule wants to wander all over and doesn't know what a straight line is. So to have an orderly, fruitful, harvestable field, you need to focus hard and work hard to make your rows straight. Plowing rows is the discipline, habits and attitudes that you develop. Don't give up or capitulate because it is hard now. Once you get several straight rows in, it can become easier.

3) What are you sowing? Many people sow any seed they happen to find or what is given to them. There is no conscious effort to discern what seed is best. Whatever happens to be there is what they sow. Some people may not be able to discern good from bad, because they have never established their own values. Sowing anything that comes along can make a field unproductive or fill it with weeds. For example: Are you sowing the seeds of debt because the credit card company and the government tell you to spend more since it is good for the economy, or because advertisements tell you that new things will make your life better? Are you eating more because someone asked you to super-size your meal, and so you did? Are you just watching any TV program because you deserve to relax after a hard day? Do you avoid talking or spending time with your spouse or children because your boss tells you work is more important? Are you placing all your dreams on your financial condition because that is what everyone else is doing? Do you reply in anger because it is easier than practicing kindness or patience? Do you let your kids watch anything on TV or the Internet because it is too much effort to monitor? Do you ever tell your kids, "No, we will not do another sport or that activity you so desire," or do you just give in so that you don't have to argue? What attitude are you sowing?

4) Are you pulling the weeds out? A good farmer doesn't just plant and then wait until harvest to see what he or she grew. No, the farmer knows that weeds need to be pulled so that the good crop can grow most effectively. Weeds compete for soil nutrients, water and root space. Do you ever examine your life and say, "I need to change this habit or attitude," and then begin to do so? Do you let others influence you when you should focus on the good crop? What weeds do you need to start pulling? What is keeping you from starting today?

5) Are you watering or fertilizing your crops? A farmer knows that planting and weeding are not the only two things that need to be done for the crop to grow. Good crops also need water and fertilizer. What are you doing to build upon the good foundations

of your life: books, seminars, church, exercise, saving money or other wholesome activities? Are you working on a continuous improvement program or just hoping that the rain will fall and you will get a good crop? Are you letting your kids get away with things instead of telling them "no"? Do you require first-time obedience, or do you negotiate with your kids on everything? Are you watering your family life or just letting it get by? When was the last time you: went away with your spouse to focus on your marriage? Took your kids to breakfast? Did something that would build a relationship?

Recently, I took my oldest daughter off for a three-day weekend. We got to spend great time together, relax, listen, discuss and just enjoy each other. This gave us opportunity to sow good seed, water and even do a little weeding in our relationship. Another area that needed weeding was credit cards. Last year my family began paying off debt and tossing the cards into the trash. What a feeling of freedom we now have!

In mid-life or the latter stages of life, we will reap the harvest from the efforts we have given. Will you enjoy your harvest or be filled with pain and tears? The choice is yours, and it must be made daily. Putting off making the right decisions is actually making the wrong decisions. Every decision you make, good or bad, is plowing a row in your field, sowing a seed or irrigating. These early decisions can be corrected, but the longer you wait, the more difficult it is. Don't wait until it is too late! Act now! Be careful and attentive to all your fields, all the areas of your life. Farmers who are not attentive may reap a wonderful harvest in one field and leave desolation in another.

Faith

Isaiah 28: 24 – *"When a farmer plows for planting, does he plow continually? Does he keep on breaking up and harrowing the soil?"*

Joel 1: 11 – *"Despair, you farmers, wail, you vine growers; grieve for the wheat and the barley, because the harvest of the field is destroyed."*

James 5: 7 – *"Be patient, then, brothers, until the Lord's coming. See how the farmer waits for the land to yield its valuable crop and how patient he is for the autumn and spring rains."*

Proverbs 11: 18 – *"The wicked man earns deceptive wages, but he who sows righteousness reaps a sure reward."*

Ecclesiastes 11: 6 – *"Sow your seed in the morning, and at evening let not your hands be idle, for you do not know which will succeed, whether this or that, or whether both will do equally well."*

Living life is hard work. The temptation is to just live to get by. In our own strength, we may think we are doing well, but all the harvest will be judged by the Creator. Are you sowing seeds that will last? As in the passage from Joel, is your harvest one that is long-lasting, eternal, or will it quickly be destroyed? Are you living your life according your Farmer's Almanac or the Creator's Almanac?

I read this _ _ _ _ _ _ times this week.

Less is More

My attitude about one area of my life was dramatically changed two years ago during a lunch conversation with a friend. We were discussing our lives, careers, goals and desires. He shared with me that he was actually thinking of downsizing, buying a smaller house. His reason was that his mortgage owned him and he had bought in to the lie that having more is better.

We talked about what having more means. Having more means you have to take care of more things, have more responsibilities and have more stress. The more things we acquire, the more they begin to own us versus our owning them.

This conversation was just at the right time. I had been looking at some land and was considering a mortgage to purchase it. After that discussion, I realized that owning more would actually tie me down, add stress and add more responsibility. What I thought would make me happy actually would begin to rule me.

That day, I began to change my attitude about acquiring more things and my true need for them, especially big things. I realized that we don't always need a bigger house or a new car.

Advertisers Want You to be Discontent

If you look at the goal of an advertiser, it is to make you dissatisfied with what you have and to then believe that what the ad offers will make you happy. Advertising is making us a bunch of discontented, never-satisfied people. "I've got to have just one more thing, and then I will be happy."

Does more really bring happiness? Does more actually relieve stress? From my observations, more brings more stress, responsibilities, worries, headaches and discontentment.

Less _IS_ More

Less is actually more. Having less lets you be free. You have fewer worries, less to protect, less to finance. A bigger house has never really made someone truly happy in the long run. Maybe it looks impressive on the outside, but the desire for a bigger house was really driven by an attitude of discontentment. "I can't be happy with what I have; I need more."

Americans are living that attitude every day. Look at the credit card debt. Typically a couple's first house was not their dream home. Now the first house is big and has a 30-year mortgage. Examine your attitude – what are you striving for?

Examine your life and ask yourself, "Where can I have less, get rid of some things? Where can I simplify my life?" Simplifying your life may be done by simply being satisfied with what you have, i.e. contentment. Simplifying your life can be done by examining what your dreams are and then asking the question, "Will this really make me happy? What are the cons of having more?"

If you want more, spend it gaining a deeper, more vibrant marriage. Get more in relationships. Get more in better health. Get more by giving to your neighbor or the downtrodden.

Faith

Proverbs 28: 25 – *"A greedy man stirs up dissension, but he who trusts in the LORD will prosper."*

Ezekiel 33: 31 – *"My people come to you, as they usually do, and sit before you to listen to your words, but they do not put them into practice. With their mouths they express devotion, but their hearts are greedy for unjust gain."*

Romans 13: 9 – *"The commandments, 'Do not commit adultery,' 'Do not murder,' 'Do not steal,' 'Do not covet,' and whatever other commandment there may be, are summed up in this one rule: 'Love your neighbor as yourself.'"*

If you are seeking meaning in life from more things, ask God to help you be satisfied with what he has given you. Ask God to help you look to help another, not add to yourself.

I read this _ _ _ _ _ _ _ times this week.

Seeking Significance

Everyone wants to have significance in his or her life. People seek it in many ways. Some seek significance in acquiring things such as cars, houses, toys, clothes or antiques. Many times they are measuring themselves against another and thinking, "I have more, so therefore I have significance." Others are thinking, "Just one more thing, and I will be fulfilled." Some seek significance in a hobby or a large possession: "My airplane, boat, beach house or model trains make me feel good." Still others seek significance in a hobby, work, a specific title or how much money they make. Many parents seek significance in raising their children. Some seek it in service to others via church, a social club, or a charity.

Searching for Meaning

People seeking significance are really seeking meaning to their life. They are looking for one or more things that give them a feeling of value. The pursuit of value is a feeling that "I am valuable because I am giving value or have value."

Unfortunately, few people find lasting significance, because their pursuit of significance is really about them. They are doing the things they do to make themselves feel or look better. It is amazing how much money is given to charity at someone's death but not while they are living. They sought significance from their money while alive but wanted to be remembered for giving in their death. Why not give the same amount away while you are alive?

What Legacy do You Want to Leave?

How you seek significance not only affects you, but it also affects your children and their children. Your children watch and model what you do. They then pass that value on to their kids. No matter what you teach, your actions will always carry more meaning and be copied and applied long before anything you say is applied. That is your legacy.

True Significance is in Relationships

True significance is found when your focus is taken off yourself and is focused on another. Giving, serving and helping another for the sake of the other person enable you to feel and have significance. Why? God made us that way. When we do things for our benefit, no matter how benevolent they are, we don't truly feel completely fulfilled. We may feel good in the short run, but it is the long run that counts.

Few people have ever said on their deathbed that working longer or having more stuff would have made their life so much better. In the end, what gives meaning to life are the positive, others-focused relationships we have. Are you a taker or a giver?

How do you develop good relationships? It first begins with developing good character. How do you develop good character? It begins by determining what character traits you want to develop or improve and working on them each day, week and month.

I have mentioned setting monthly goals. Have you? I have mentioned using affirmations to change an attitude. Are you? Just acknowledging that you need to change is not changing. To develop a better character, you have to take action. Set a monthly goal; write down the affirmation that will help you become a better person.

Read some books that build character. Listen to life development CDs or podcasts by people such as Zig Ziglar, Jim Rohn, Dennis Waitley and Brian Tracey. Get involved in a Bible study. Go help a neighbor. Get involved in a local charity.

Faith

Psalms 1: 1-3 – *"Blessed is the man who does not walk in the counsel of the wicked or stand in the way of sinners or sit in the seat of mockers. But his delight is in the law of the LORD, and on his law he meditates day and night. He is like a tree planted by streams of water, which yields its fruit in season and whose leaf does not wither. Whatever he does prospers."*

Psalms 28: 7-9 – *"The LORD is my strength and my shield; my heart trusts in him, and I am helped. My heart leaps for joy and I will give thanks to him in song. The LORD is the strength of his people, a fortress of salvation for his anointed one. Save your people and bless your inheritance; be their shepherd and carry them forever."*

John 10: 10 – *"The thief comes only to steal and kill and destroy; I came that they may have life, and have it abundantly."*

In the past sections I have mentioned that life is like a wheel with 7 spokes. At the center of the wheel is a hub. In most people's lives, the hub is themselves, and that is where they struggle for significance. God made us to have Him as the hub where our lives are centered, living in a relationship with Him. God as the center of life gives us meaning and gives meaning to the things we do. He made us to have abundant life, a significant life, which can only be lasting when our life is controlled by Him. Seek His counsel; stand in His way; do not mock truth.

Jesus said, "I have come to give abundant life." Have you accepted Jesus as the center of your hub? Acknowledgment is not enough. It is a matter of control. Who is going to be in charge of your life, you or Jesus?

I read this _ _ _ _ _ _ _ times this week.

Dream Enabler
or Dream Taker?

Have you ever wondered how a person becomes successful? I even wonder how someone becomes a failure. Typically, behind success and failure, there are certain attitudes and as well as particular input from others.

Attitudes for Success

The key attitudes for success are perseverance, picking yourself up one more time, focusing on the goal, and always intentionally putting positive thoughts in your mind.

What about the input from others? If you could see behind a person's success or failures, there is typically another person who was encouraging or discouraging the person. They were either sowing good seeds or bad seeds in building the right or wrong attitudes.

Are you a dream enabler – i.e. an encourager – or a dream taker? Do you intentionally build someone up? Or do you carelessly sow seeds of discouragement? It is always easier to see why NOT to do something than to figure out a way **to** do something. It is easier to take a dream away from another than to help that person build the dream or make it a reality.

Possibility Thinker or Negativity Thinker?

How would you be defined: possibility thinker or negativity thinker? To help a person succeed, you need to be an encourager, helping your friend, family member or co-worker see the possibilities, even in difficult situations. For most people, it is easier to see the negative and focus on the negative, telling the other, "It can't be done," or "It's not worth it." This negativity takes a value system – values of cynicism or skepticism – and attempts to transfer it to another person. This is destructive.

Changing Others

For you possibility thinkers, avoid negative thinkers. Don't allow their bad seeds to take root. Spread positive thoughts to others. You may convert someone from a negative thinker to a positive thinker. Give good thoughts; make someone's day.

Negative thinkers come in many colors, including people who worry all the time (they will go to great lengths telling you why it is OK or good for them to worry), and sedentary people who see no reason to move forward. They say, "Life is comfortable here." Much misery is caused by inaction. A person knows what to do, but doesn't do it. Most stay in their miserable situation because of negative thinking.

Positive thinkers and positive encouragers enable others to seek and achieve their dreams. Be a dream-giver to someone. Tell your kids "yes" vs. always telling them "no." Instead of saying, "No, it can't be done," ask the person, "How would you approach this issue or solve the problem?" Help bring the best out in others by positively challenging them instead of negatively judging their ideas or actions.

The Power of Questions

Positive people ask questions instead of just making judgments. They look for the possibilities or undiscovered opportunities. Asking a question enables new discoveries. Negative comments just bury the idea or issue.

138

Faith

Matthew 19: 26 – *"Jesus looked at them and said, 'With man this is impossible, but with God all things are possible.'"*

Mark 9: 23 – *"'If you can?'" said Jesus. 'Everything is possible for him who believes.'"*

Many times we feel defeated because we rely on ourselves and see no possible good. We may not see anything positive in a situation. With God, all things are possible, and all things can work for His good. What is lacking is our faith in God. Nothing is impossible for Him.

If you are facing a tough situation, don't go to God last. Go to God first, seeking his deliverance or asking Him to change your attitude toward the situation. Ask Him to help you see the good, the possibilities, not the negatives. Ask that His will be done.

All too often, we rely on ourselves and only go to God when we feel we can't do it on our own. In reality this is a prideful, self-sufficient attitude. We are really viewing God as a magic genie only to be called on when in time of need. We are not putting our faith in the Creator of the Universe!

James 4: 5-6 – *"Or do you think Scripture says without reason that the spirit he caused to live in us envies intensely? But he gives us more grace. That is why Scripture says: 'God opposes the proud but gives grace to the humble.'"*

I read this _ _ _ _ _ _ _ times this week.

Having Endurance

How do you create endurance? Is endurance an attitude, character trait or physical quality? Yes, on all counts!

Endurance is first an attitude. The attitude is developed in several ways: being goal-focused, having a view of the big picture, and being tough-minded. The attitude of endurance is developed over our life span, starting with little things and growing as we grow.

Goals-Focused

The attitude of endurance is being goal-focused. It looks beyond the circumstances and focuses on the goal to be achieved. It looks beyond the circumstances to the big picture. The more clearly defined the goal, the easier it is for a person to focus on the goal instead of the circumstances. The goal must be *your* goal, not someone else's, and it needs to be specific, measurable, attainable, realistic and tangible. If you are struggling and want to quit, go back and see how important the goal is. Is it worth having endurance to achieve the goal? If you are not sure, re-examine the value of the goal.

Character

Endurance is also a character trait stemming from an overall attitude of "I am tough; I don't quit. I go the long haul." A person who continually shows endurance in circumstances has practiced developing the right attitudes so that endurance is now part of him or her. This person is now characterized as being a person who endures. How do you develop this character? It comes through practice. You practice endurance by placing yourself or finding yourself in situations that are tough. When you feel like quitting, you give it just a little extra, and you hold on just a little longer. You tell yourself, "I can handle this. I can endure this." And when you have handled it, you congratulate yourself so that you can do it again the next time: "See, I knew I could do that!"

A runner trains for a race by running a little extra each time he or she runs. Endurance as a character trait is developed the same way. Parents, teaching your children endurance while they are young is one of the greatest gifts you can give them. Making them stay in the game when they feel like quitting, or making them finish the job even though they are tired, is a wonderful gift. It seems hard on them now, but you are developing character.

Our society is training people to quit when the going gets tough. A self-absorbed generation has little endurance.

Physical Endurance

Some people are just tougher than others, so it is hard to compare yourself to someone else. We tend to always compare ourselves to someone who is far better than us and see ourselves as lacking. Focus on yourself and on moving toward *your* goal, not another's. Developing physical endurance is much the same as developing endurance of character. It comes with practice. Push yourself a little farther each time. Exercise, focus on the project at hand; deny yourself in order to get a little tougher. Take the stairs instead of the elevator. Park far away from the store and walk. The little things do matter, for they help build the attitude and the character.

Endurance in Life

A key to endurance in life is keeping yourself in shape to have endurance. This requires continually working on your attitude, using self-talk such as, "I am a person of endurance. I have a character of endurance. I am an enduring person." It requires continually viewing your goals, reassessing or redefining your goals and identifying your values, what really matters in the long run. Having an accountability or support partner helps you endure. Having hope and a higher purpose enables you endure. Lastly, keeping yourself physically fit enables you to have greater endurance. Through exercise, your body is used to having stress on it, so a little hardship is not unknown.

Those who don't take care of their bodies have a tendency to quit when the going gets tough, because they are not used to tough going. The same goes with attitude. If you are not a little tough on yourself in going the extra mile or enduring mildly to moderately difficult circumstances, when it gets really tough, you will fold or the situation will be very painful.

Faith

Romans 15: 4-5 — *"For everything that was written in the past was written to teach us, so that through endurance and the encouragement of the Scriptures we might have hope. May the God who gives endurance and encouragement give you a spirit of unity among yourselves as you follow Christ Jesus."*

Colossians 1: 10-12 — *"And we pray this in order that you may live a life worthy of the Lord and may please him in every way: bearing fruit in every good work, growing in the knowledge of God, being strengthened with all power according to his glorious might so that you may have great endurance and patience, and joyfully giving thanks to the Father, who has qualified you to share in the inheritance of the saints in the kingdom of light."*

If you are going through a tough time, ask God to help you with developing a spirit of endurance. Ask him to give you hope, for with hope comes endurance. Ask him to give you a heart of compassion or service or generosity.

If you see someone having a hard time, give him or her some help. Many times we say, "I will pray for you," but what the person really needs is not prayer but some actual help.

Many times a person endures a hardship because others were there to support them. Be a support to another! Love your neighbor as yourself.

I read this _ _ _ _ _ _ _ times this week.

Entertaining Discernment

Do you discriminate? I do. Everyone does. *Discriminate* means to make a choice, to decide between two options. The second question is, do you use discernment when you discriminate? *Discernment* is to decide between right and wrong.

Today's society is very careful to not use the words *right* and *wrong* in the same sentence, for implying there is a right and a wrong means that people could be making bad choices or doing bad things. The popular sentiment encourages us to experiment, to see reality from our own perspective. We are regularly told that whatever you do, if it gives you meaning, it is OK to do it.

Many argue that telling someone "no" harms them – it hinders their personal expression and their growth as a human being. To imply that there is a right and a wrong means that one person could be wrong in his choices and that another could be right in her choices. A wrong choice leads to bad consequences.

Entertainment

Let's examine where discernment should be used, not in the big issues, but just in what we consider a little or inconsequential issue – entertainment.

Have you ever given much thought to the TV shows or movies you watch? Most people do. They give thought to the quality of entertainment: "I don't like that program" or "That movie stunk." Why did it stink? Typically, the judgment was based upon the entertainment value: the quality of action, the quality of production, the sound or the excitement, but not on the moral value.

I challenge you to now start looking at two things in your entertainment: the first is quality in a moral context. The second is quantity – how much time and money do you spend on entertainment?

What is the Moral Message?

Using discernment in entertainment takes a moral position and asks, "Does the message of this entertainment build up others or tear them down?" "Does the message of this entertainment promote the good and welfare of another, or does the main character use other people to get what he/she wants?" "Does this entertainment promote violence, or does it promote peace?" "Does the entertainment promote a faithful marriage, or does it promote promiscuous sex?"

Other important questions to ask include, "Does this entertainment create a better society or create or reflect a worse society?" "Does the entertainment show you the long-term consequences of the choices made?" Typically entertainment does not do this; the theme is often on the short-term "fun" or feeling of the moment. Rarely shown, if ever, are the destroyed marriages, the depressed life, the bankrupt person.

Habit vs. Simple Pleasure?

The second issue regarding entertainment is frequency and priority. What priority does entertainment take in your life? How much money or time do you spend entertaining yourself? Do you use entertainment as a way to avoid other things or people with which you really should be engaged? Do you use entertainment to escape responsibility?

Too many people come home and click on the TV and check out from their family. Kids come home and get on the Internet and check out from interacting with Mom or Dad. Husbands come home, sit on the couch and check out instead of talking with their wife, helping get dinner ready or helping kids with their homework. In many cases, the TV and Internet have replaced family communication.

Typically the entertainment we choose is one that requires little to no thinking. It has no purpose except to "amuse" us. One definition of *amuse* is "to divert the attention so as to deceive."

By not engaging your mind, those who create the entertainment are determining what you will think about, what values you will have. We are being deceived.

Entertainment can be like the frog in the kettle. Slowly turn up the heat, and the frog will be boiled without ever jumping out.

Assessing Your Own Entertainment Habits

Many years ago, my wife and I became aware of the impact that entertainment was having on us, our language, our thoughts, even our time spent together. My wife and I started cutting back on TV during the week and started using more discretion in the movies we watched. For the shows and movies we do watch, we discuss the theme and purpose. We don't "just watch" to be entertained. We now try to discern what the writer, producer, actor were trying to communicate. We even try to use entertainment as an opportunity to engage with each other and with the family.

Parents, a great exercise with your kids is to talk about the movies or TV shows they watch and what moral or immoral lessons are being taught. Talk with them about the long-term consequences of the actions that the characters are taking. Discuss with them the behaviors of actors in the sitcom. Are they loving their neighbor as themselves, or are they tearing another down to make themselves feel good? Are they crude, rude and distasteful? Discuss the maturity of the actor or actress in the situation. Ask if the actors used good judgment, and why or why not?

Faith

Proverbs 27: 12 – *"The prudent see danger and take refuge, but the simple keep going and suffer for it."*

The prudent person is the one who uses discernment. He judges right from wrong. He/she asks the question, "Where will my actions, thoughts or attitudes lead me? Will the long-term effects be good or bad for me? Will they be good or bad for those around me?" The prudent tells himself, "Just because I can do it doesn't make it right to do or wholesome for me to do."

The prudent evaluates his or her life regarding entertainment and asks, "Do I place too much emphasis on entertainment? Am I putting garbage in my mind? Am I using the opportunity to teach my children moral values? Am I letting myself or my family slip backwards in our relationships, moral character, health or finances because of our entertainment habits?"

The simple don't ask these questions. The simple just follow their habits because, for the moment, it is enjoyable. The simple suffer in the long run.

Colossians 3: 5-8 – *"Put to death, therefore, whatever belongs to your earthly nature: sexual immorality, impurity, lust, evil desires and greed, which is idolatry. Because of these, the wrath of God is coming. You used to walk in these ways, in the life you once lived. But now you must rid yourselves of all such things as these: anger, rage, malice, slander and filthy language from your lips."*

I read this _ _ _ _ _ _ _ times this week.

Forgiveness

Forgive – Do you know how to forgive another or receive forgiveness?

Forgive Another

All of us have been wronged in some way during our lives. Some are minor insults; other times there are major hurts. How does one get past a hurtful time in his or her life? The first step is forgiveness. Forgiveness is very hard, especially if you have deep and painful emotional, financial or other types of scars. Forgiveness is hard, especially when the offending person has not acknowledged that what he or she did to you was wrong or even gloated in what he or she did to you. Forgiveness is hard and painful when the other person did it to intentionally hurt you.

Not Forgiving

Have you ever thought of the power of holding a grudge or a deep resentment or even hate when not forgiving another person? You feel powerful that you are actually doing something productive to get back at the other person. In reality, the only power that is being exerted is on you. It is a destructive power, destroying you from the inside out.

Truly forgiving someone frees you. It takes a huge burden off you, from the inside out. It enables you to look at life afresh, from a new perspective. Forgiveness allows you to look to the future in a whole new way.

Stuck in the Past?

People who don't forgive are stuck in the past. They can't move forward because the pain of the past is too great. Many people use their past experiences as their identity. Their grudge becomes who they are.

In reality, the only person you destroy when you don't forgive is yourself. If you can't forgive, ask God to help you. Not forgiving has no power over the offending party; it just ruins you.

Receiving Forgiveness

Do you have trouble receiving forgiveness? Do you ever think, "I am not worthy to receive forgiveness?" Many think that kind of attitude is a humble attitude. But in actuality, an attitude of "I am not worthy to be forgiven" is a very proud attitude. It says, "I can do better, so don't forgive me until I do better." The emphasis is on "I."

Receiving forgiveness means focusing on the other person and being thankful that the person does forgive you. It is accepting the other person's grace. A person who truly accepts forgiveness then works to become a better person. He or she is humble and thankful. Many times pride gets in the way of us being forgiven.

Faith

Psalms 130: 3-5 – *"If you, O LORD, kept a record of sins, O Lord, who could stand? But with you there is forgiveness; therefore you are feared. I wait for the LORD, my soul waits, and in his word I put my hope."*

Colossians 1: 13-15 – *"For he has rescued us from the dominion of darkness and brought us into the kingdom of the Son he loves, in whom we have redemption, the forgiveness of sins."*

Only in Christ are we truly, completely forgiven for all things. Have you received that forgiveness?

Forgiving Others

Matthew 6: 12 from the Lord's Prayer – *"Forgive us our debts, as we also have forgiven our debtors."*

Colossians 3: 13 – *"Bear with each other and forgive whatever grievances you may have against one another. Forgive as the Lord forgave you."*

In Christ you have total forgiveness. Are you holding back giving that to another?

I read this _ _ _ _ _ _ _ times this week.

Asking for Forgiveness

Have you ever really screwed up, then wanted to defend yourself instead of just asking for forgiveness and to make things right? I know I have. Recently, I have seen two personal illustrations of a big mistake turning into a huge screw-up. Both of these scenarios were when a person did something wrong, and instead of asking forgiveness and seeking to make amends, he or she tried to cover it up. The cover-up became bigger than the initial event and really messed up that person's life and all those involved. Instead of just one person going down, many people were affected because of the cover-up. Bad choices do have bad consequences.

Life Leaders are people who recognize that they do make mistakes, miss deadlines, and at times don't fulfill promises, but these people seek to make amends. Life Leaders are people who will eat humble pie, admit they are wrong, and then work to make the situation better. Life Leaders ask for forgiveness.

Seeking true forgiveness is not saying "I'm sorry," for "I'm sorry" is only from the speaker's perspective. That statement is not about the person being offended, but about the offender. Seeking true forgiveness is saying, "I am sorry for having done this wrong (whatever it is) to you; it hurt you. I ask your forgiveness; will you forgive me?" Also, if needed, "I will do this _____ to make it right."

Seeking true forgiveness is focusing on how you offended the other person and what needs to be done to restore the relationship. Seeking true forgiveness is others-focused and is relationship-focused. Those who defend their actions or try to cover them up are only focused on themselves. Being focused only on yourself alienates the other person.

When teaching your kids to how say "I'm sorry" for an offense, teach them the principle of identifying the offense and truly asking forgiveness. A quick "I'm sorry" typically is just an appeasement to Mom or Dad to get the parent off the child's back. Some people may need hours or even a day to contemplate their offense before they seek restoration of a relationship. Give that child opportunity to contemplate and realize the degree of his or her offense. If necessary, this opportunity may be enhanced through measures such as time out, taking away privileges, extra chores, working for the other person, fixing the problem or working to pay off the offense. Once the child truly understands his or her wrongdoing or offense, then repentance and restoration can begin. Without acknowledgement of guilt, there cannot be true forgiveness.

152

Faith

Proverbs 28: 13 – *"He who conceals his sins does not prosper, but whoever confesses them and renounces them finds mercy."*

In the story of David and Bathsheba, David tried to cover up his sin of adultery with Bathsheba and ended up having her husband killed. As a result, David lost several sons and had the kingdom in turmoil. His cover-up had far greater negative consequences than the adulterous affair.

God is a God of forgiveness and invites you to confess your sin, for He will forgive you. He also encourages us to "confess our sins to another," which is the idea of seeking forgiveness from the party that you wounded.

Is there someone to whom you need to go today to ask forgiveness and make restitution?

I read this _ _ _ _ _ _ _ times this week.

Facing Adversity

Everyone in his or her life will face some type of adversity. Right now, I am trying to keep a new business alive. It is tough going, and the reality is that only 1 out of 10 new businesses make it. But with that information, I have a choice. Do I want to be in the 90th percentile or the 10th percentile?

I am reading a book by Jim Collins called *Good to Great*. His question is, "What makes a good company move to become a great company?"

Two of the key components are attitude and addressing reality.

Attitude of Hope

The attitude that enables a company or a person to survive the bad times and even grow is "retaining a faith that you will prevail in the end, regardless of the difficulties."

This attitude gives a person, family or a company the staying power to endure the worst of circumstances. This attitude, writes Collins, enabled Admiral Jim Stockdale to survive 8 years of imprisonment and being tortured over 20 times in the infamous "Hanoi Hilton" during the Vietnam War.

Confronting Reality

Collins quotes Stockdale as saying that the other key determinant in overcoming adversity is that you must "confront the most brutal facts of your current reality, no matter what they might be."

Confronting the most brutal facts takes your head out of the sand. Confronting the facts says, "I or we must do something about these facts." Confronting those brutal facts may be maintaining a positive attitude no matter what your circumstances. It may mean working twice as hard to get to the same place as another person. Confronting the adversity may mean you have to work two jobs.

The difference in true leaders and people who just "hope" for the best is that true leaders actually look at their situation and ask, "What can I do to make things better? What do I have to do to change the situation?" True leaders don't just look to others to deliver them, nor do they look to blame others for their circumstances. The circumstances are what they are, and the leader deals with them.

A true leader does maintain the attitude that he/she will prevail in the end. That faith and hope keep a person going, even in the most difficult circumstances.

Life Leaders come out of these hard circumstances as stronger and more wholesome people.

Those who remember Apollo 13, with both the tragedy and the triumph, can see these principles applied. The astronauts never gave up hope, and they believed they would make it back to Earth. But they also faced reality and worked hard to ensure that they did make it back.

In facing adversity, do you just sit down and think the worst? Do you blame others for the hardships? Do you see yourself as a victim?

Faith

Hebrews 11: 1 – *"Now faith is being sure of what we hope for and certain of what we do not see."*

Hebrews 11: 8-14 – *"By faith Abraham, when called to go to a place he would later receive as his inheritance, obeyed and went, even though he did not know where he was going. By faith he made his home in the Promised Land like a stranger in a foreign country; he lived in tents, as did Isaac and Jacob, who were heirs with him of the same promise. For he was looking forward to the city with foundations whose architect and builder is God.*

By faith Abraham, even though he was past age – and Sarah herself was barren – was enabled to become a father because he considered him faithful who had made the promise. And so from this one man, and he as good as dead, came descendants as numerous as the stars in the sky and as countless as the sand on the seashore."

No matter what the circumstances, God is faithful. He gives us examples of people such as Abraham, who exercised faith in the most difficult of circumstances.

God can enable you to change, but He also requires you to confront the realities of who you are. First, confess your sins and repent. After having a change of heart and mind, then seek the best, and be ready to receive forgiveness and to be changed. The first step in confronting your situation is to ask God for help and believe that you will receive it.

I read this _ _ _ _ _ _ _ times this week.

Lessons Learned From a Dog

In the fall of 2008, I had a very sad day. I had to put my faithful friend, Freckles, our dog, to sleep because he was very sick. The story of our dog is a story about change as much as anything else – change for me and the dog.

Being Secure

Freckles was a beautiful Brittany spaniel who we rescued when he was about 3 years old. Freckles was non-aggressive and very friendly. We brought him home, but he exhibited the strangest behavior – he would not bark. Matter of fact, he would not bark at all for about 4 months. Our friends would laugh at our new dog, thinking him quite strange. Then one day, he barked – and started barking regularly. I believe this was due to his feeling of security and belonging. Originally, he was not sure of his security, being a part of a pack – in this case being a permanent part of our family – so he had no reason to protect what was not his. Of course, he marked everything outside!

Lesson learned – If people feel insecure, they will not exhibit their normal behavior or be themselves. Make people feel secure in your relationships – no manipulation, no posturing for position. Give no negative or derogatory remarks; encourage others.

Parameters Deliver Freedom

Freckles thought he was the alpha male and would not sit, stay, come or do anything else. In his mind, he was boss until.... we went to dog school. As the Dog Whisperer says, the dog is fine; the owners need training. I quickly established who the alpha male was and who was not. Freckles went through lots of obedience training and became an enjoyable dog. He became more relaxed, was fun to have, and knew his place. We could go for a walk without a leash. He would run, chase squirrels, but come when I called and heel when commanded. He gained twice as much freedom by being obedient.

Lesson learned – People as well as dogs need parameters to feel secure and know they belong. Left alone with no parameters, they make rules for themselves, which is destructive. Children need guidelines, stricter at first and less when they show responsibility. Responsibility leads to freedom.

Greeting Reflects Attitude

Whenever we had someone come over, Freckles almost wiggled out of his skin with excitement, thinking that the visitor had come to see him. He made visitors feel quite welcomed. When I would come home, he would be lying at the top of the stairs and would give me the happiest warm greeting, with a lick. If he was in his box, he would jump up to greet me. Freckles' greeting always showed his positive, happy attitude.

Lesson learned – Greet people with enthusiasm; make them feel welcome and make them feel that you are glad to meet them. Freckles used a lick, but a handshake and a warm smile and "Hello," "Pleased to meet you" or "Good morning" would work better for humans. Your greeting reflects your attitude.

Fun is Good

Freckles loved to play tug of war with his pull toy in the yard every day. He was not happy until *I* (being the alpha male) gave him attention. He would bug me until I played with him. Then he would be quite content, calm and obedient. He would pull, shake, growl as we tugged. If he won by pulling the toy out of my hand, he would run around the yard in a triumphant manner. He would then return to tug some more unless he could entice us to chase him.

Lesson learned – Have fun, let down your guard, take time out. Lesson for Dads and Moms – play with your kids. Stop what you are doing and just get physical with them. I still get into tickle matches or light wrestling with my teenagers. A few weeks ago, we wrestled for about 20 minutes in the ocean, all laughing. (They almost drowned me.) We all agreed that the time in the water was the most fun time at the beach. Play builds relationships better than any other activity. Play also makes people feel secure.

Forgiveness Maintains Relationships

Freckles at times did drive me nuts, for he loved to chase squirrels, and he also liked being inside. So, if a squirrel was in the yard, he wanted out, then back in… then out, then back in…, etc. etc. He would also get into the trash or chew up my things that were outside. I would regularly get mad at him, and many times even yelled (bad example). But he never stopped loving me and was always glad to see me.

Lesson learned – Be forgiving; no one is perfect. Forgiveness builds relationships.

A View from the Other Side

There was a time when the dog was driving me crazy, always bugging me, wanting in and then out, getting into the trash, etc. (Looking back, I can see that the problem was that the kids were not playing with him enough, so he was bored.) I was mad at the dog regularly, and the kids started harassing me about it, saying that he was just being a dog, that I was the alpha male and that he needed my attention. I did not care what Freckles' problem was; he was very annoying to me.

Then one day as I was playing with him – for he had been begging for over an hour for me to play with him – I realized that the kids would remember me always being mad at the dog. During that play time, the dog kept falling because he had arthritis in his hips. I learned two things in that play time: I was viewing the dog from only my perspective, and the dog was just being a dog. I had compassion for him, because he was slowing down in how he played, but stilled he played with all the enthusiasm and fierceness he could muster. After that day, my whole demeanor and outlook on the dog changed. I began to like the dog and treat him with extra attention. He loved me all the more.

Lesson learned – See things from other's perspective, for it may cause you to have compassion. Also, I learned that others were watching my behavior, and I would be remembered for how I acted – kindly or in anger. No matter how I justified my behavior, others would remember my actions from their perspective: a) he was mean to the dog, or b) he loved the dog. I learned to change. When Freckles died, my kids were most concerned for me, because the dog and I had become good friends. How will you be remembered by your kids, friends, co-workers, etc.?

We all can learn a lesson from a dog if we take time, are teachable and willing to reflect.

- Have Patience
- Parameters are needed
- Be enthusiastic
- Have fun; be yourself
- Be forgiving
- Others are watching
- Be empathetic

Faith

Proverbs 1: 1-5 – *"The proverbs of Solomon son of David, king of Israel: for attaining wisdom and discipline; for understanding words of insight; for acquiring a disciplined and prudent life, doing what is right and just and fair; for giving prudence to the simple, knowledge and discretion to the young – let the wise listen and add to their learning, and let the discerning get guidance – for understanding proverbs and parables, the sayings and riddles of the wise. The fear of the LORD is the beginning of knowledge, but fools despise wisdom and discipline."*

Too many times we think we have nothing to learn. It is that attitude that shows us how far we have to go or that we are a fool. Are you building your life on continual learning, or are you just coasting, believing what you hear on the news, the pundits, and the sitcoms? Are you modeling a life of continual examination and learning for your kids? Are you a good example to your spouse, friends or co-workers? Do you work on building better character? Are you open to learning from your dog?

It is amazing what you can learn from a dog if you are willing. Step out of yourself and examine yourself.

I did and was changed. ☺

Freckles – Rest in Peace.

I read this _ _ _ _ _ _ _ times this week.

Examine Your Life

What habits have you developed around instant gratification? Do you abuse credit cards? Do you get angry quickly because something did not go your way? Do you run red lights so you don't have to wait the two minutes for the light to change? Do you get mad at your computer for how long it takes to boot up?

Are you contemplating going physically further with your boyfriend or girlfriend because you just don't want to wait until you are married? Do you think, "No one waits"?

If any of these answers is "yes," a check-up on your life is greatly needed. I suspect relationships might be in danger of becoming shallow or stressed. I suspect there are other issues, too, that are gnawing at you. Some instant gratification decisions are life-changing... for the worst. You can't retrieve what you have lost. You can't give back the disease. You can't take back hateful words.

The root cause is lack of patience and a belief that life is not satisfying unless you get everything you want, NOW.

Faith

Ecclesiastes 7: 8 – *"The end of a matter is better than its beginning, and patience is better than pride."*

Galatians 5: 22-23 – *"But the fruit of the Spirit is love, joy, peace, patience, kindness, goodness, faithfulness, gentleness and self-control. Against such there is no law."*

Ask God to give you self-control and patience. Ask Him to help you see beyond the moment. Ask for wisdom to see the bad side of the decision you are about to make.

Ask yourself, "Do I really need this? Will my life really be better?" Ask your child the same question.

I read this _ _ _ _ _ _ _ times this week.

Enjoying Life in a Richer Way – Thankfulness

Have you ever wondered how some people seem to enjoy life more than others? It seems these people just don't have all the difficulties others do. Or if they do have difficulties, they just are "unique" in their ability to cope.

I disagree with those two premises. I have found in my own life that the secret to enjoying life in a richer way is to have an attitude of gratefulness, to have a spirit of thanksgiving. When I have not been grateful, I typically have focused on one thing not going my way. I became down and saw things in a negative way. When I am grateful, EVERYTHING looks better.

Looking at the negative in life has become so easy, a habit for many people. Every advertisement tells you that your life is not complete unless you buy this product, smell a certain way, get your tummy tucked, own a bigger house, car, boat, etc. or get a new spouse. Do you have the best insurance? If not, how can you be happy? Quack, quack.

It is the American way to want and get more, the idea being, "The more I have, the happier I will be." Unfortunately, that is not the case. Why does it seem that some of the poorest people are the happiest? How can they enjoy life when they have so little?

Attitude is the Barometer

The answer lies in one's perspective.

If you are always wanting more, coveting what your neighbor has or seeing how someone else is getting a better deal, wife, house, job, etc., then you will look at life with a tainted eye. "You are not getting enough."

If you focus your whole happiness on things going your way, you will be miserable, possibly depressed, and you can become cynical. We often put so much emphasis on one area that it taints us in all areas. We can't see anything good in any situation, when, in actuality, everything is great. Circumstances are just not working out as we would prefer.

For instance, we may be thinking, "We pay the bills but don't have enough money. My job is not secure. My wife does not meet all my needs. My kids could be better."

But if you look at what you do have and are grateful, you will be freed to enjoy what you have. It will free you up to see how truly blessed you are. If you are in America, you are truly blessed, no matter how bad your circumstances.

Unfortunately, having a grateful heart is not so easy. As mentioned, advertisements tell us not to be grateful but to want more. We are taught to look ahead for more and not around or behind us to see what others don't have compared to us. Having a grateful heart actually requires a person to say, "I have enough."

Enjoying Life

Developing a grateful heart truly enables you to enjoy life so much more. A grateful heart enables you to take the focus off yourself and place it on helping another. People who have felt they have achieved meaningful significance in life report that significance is typically most apparent when they are helping another.

How does one develop a grateful heart? First, start each day by saying out loud what you are thankful for. It may be a good night's rest, a meal, a job, etc. "I am thankful for my family." Others need to hear you being thankful. It will then be contagious.

Second, tell yourself that you are a thankful, grateful person. Do it as a vocal affirmation: "I am a grateful person. Life is good."

If you are in a difficult situation, find something good in it and write or say the positive. If nothing is good in that situation, find other things that are good and talk about them.

The overall point is to look for the good; make a conscious decision every day to see the good in your life – your spouse, your kids, your job, etc., then tell another. Get your family involved in seeing the good. Discuss how grateful you are at a meal.

Family

In our family, we just started the "I am thankful" bowl. When one of us thinks of something he or she is thankful for, the person writes it on a small piece of paper and places it in the bowl. The bowl is now starting to fill up. We are going to start reading these at a meal.

Help your kids go beyond being thankful for things and situations that just benefit them. Help them be thankful for other people and other people's uniqueness. Help them be thankful even for adversity, for it makes us stronger.

Talk about being thankful and having a grateful heart.

Lastly, check your words. Do more complaints come out of your mouth than blessings or positive statements? Are you cynical, looking for the negative? Do you easily find fault with another?

Being thankful or grateful requires the right attitude. The right attitudes are developed as a habit, as are the wrong attitudes.

Faith

God is good and has given us rich blessings. Focus on giving a blessing to another in word, deed, or gift. Show your gratitude by sharing.

Give thanks to God – Psalms 106: 1 – *"Praise the LORD! Oh give thanks to the LORD, for He is good; For His loving kindness is everlasting."*

Giving thanks for others – 2 Thessalonians 1: 3 – *"We ought always to give thanks to God for you, brethren, as is only fitting, because your faith is greatly enlarged, and the love of each one of you toward one another grows ever greater."*

Give thanks in everything – I Thessalonians 5: 18 – *"In everything give thanks; for this is God's will for you in Christ Jesus."*

If you are having trouble being grateful, ask God for help. Ask Him to open your eyes up to His goodness and the goodness that is all around you.

I read this _ _ _ _ _ _ _ times this week.

Christmas...Why Bother?

"'Tis the season to be jolly." Are you? Why bother with such a stress-filled time of year? There is too much stress trying to get just the right gift, please your family, put on a facade to show that you get along, etc.

As the Grinch described Christmas:

> "The Grinch hated Christmas,
> the whole Christmas season.
> Oh, please don't ask why,
> no one quite knows the reason....
> 'One thing I can't stand is the
> noise, noise, noise, noise!'"

Is Christmas just noise to you?

I encourage you to take a new perspective, a perspective not about you or even about others, but one that is about the origin of Christmas: The Christ Mass for the death and resurrection of Christ portrayed in the last supper.

Chris Tomlin's song "Everlasting God" helps us see the true meaning of Christmas:

Everlasting God

> Strength will rise as we wait upon the Lord;
> We will wait upon the Lord.
> We will wait upon the Lord.
>
> Our God, You reign forever
> Our hope, our Strong Deliverer —
> You are the everlasting God
> The everlasting God.
> You do not faint;
> You won't grow weary.

> You're the defender of the weak;
> You comfort those in need.
> You lift us up on wings like eagles.

Stop, reflect on these words. What do they mean?

They are clearly not about us, or about gift-giving or about holiday lights or a good warm, fuzzy feeling.

At one time Christmas was considered a holy time, but when society commercializes and denigrates the true meaning, it truly does become "meaningless." Thus, a meaningless holiday does cause stress, anxiety and pain in many. Activity without true meaning is futile.

Faith

Romans 8: 31-39 – *"What, then, shall we say in response to this? If God is for us, who can be against us? He who did not spare his own Son, but gave him up for us all – how will he not also, along with him, graciously give us all things? Who will bring any charge against those whom God has chosen? It is God who justifies. Who is he that condemns? Christ Jesus, who died – more than that, who was raised to life – is at the right hand of God and is also interceding for us. Who shall separate us from the love of Christ? Shall trouble or hardship or persecution or famine or nakedness or danger or sword? As it is written:*

'For your sake we face death all day long; we are considered as sheep to be slaughtered.'

No, in all these things we are more than conquerors through him who loved us. For I am convinced that neither death nor life, neither angels nor demons, neither the present nor the future, nor any powers, neither height nor depth, nor anything else in all creation, will be able to separate us from the love of God that is in Christ Jesus our Lord."

In Christmas we celebrate the Christ Mass. Rejoice this season, for in Christ, nothing can separate you from God's love.

Are you waiting on God? Have you not seen or experienced Him?

He has appeared. If you don't see Him, it means that you are not asking to see Him as He really is. All you have to do is ask to see Him, not on your terms, but on His. He will make Himself known.

I read this _ _ _ _ _ _ _ times this week.

Christmas Traditions

Today is the first Sunday of the Christmas season, and we got into a discussion of traditions at Sunday school. People laughed and discussed why their family tradition was fun or "funny." One of our family traditions is having a huge Christmas breakfast with Southern country ham, red eye gravy, hot biscuits, grits, eggs, bacon and lots of coffee. You need a nap after that meal. My wife has suggested changing one or two of our Christmas traditions, and my kids and I have said, "No, for we have always done it that way." That is the way the Harts celebrate Christmas. It is just the way things "should" be.

Another tradition was started thirteen years ago at Christmas time. We started inviting an "outsider" to share our family Christmas. At first it was a single elderly woman who babysat my small children. She spent 10 Christmases with us. One year we had a college student from Thailand spend a week with us, for she could not go home over the holidays. For three years a Korean student shared the holidays. For the past six years, we have had other Thai students from University of Alabama-Birmingham spend Christmas day with us. It has been so neat to share our family traditions with those who don't have a family nearby. My wife, kids and I explain why we decorate our tree a certain way, give gifts, read the Christmas story from the gospel of Luke, eat two huge meals on Christmas day, etc. We have included this person into our most intimate times. At first I thought my parents and my wife's parents would object, because none had ever done that before (i.e., there was no tradition), but they were glad to have others join us. This year our Thai friends have all graduated and gone back to Thailand. I just realized that I need to find someone else to invite to share Christmas blessings.

When reflecting on this experience, I conclude several things: Traditions are important, for they give our family a sense of identity, a sense of belonging. Traditions, whether around a holiday or other times, give stability. The second thing is that Christmas is a time to look beyond ourselves to the giver of all good things. We have truly benefited from the relationships of having others outside our immediate family participate in the Hart Christmas. It has been a joy for the whole family to share with others, especially foreigners who don't have family in America.

Keep traditions, for they are good. I also encourage you to seek out someone this year with which to share your blessings.

172

Faith

Christmas time has been made into a commercial holiday. Popular society has turned "Merry Christmas" into "Happy Holidays." From the eyes of a foreigner, many don't know that Christmas stands for "Christ Mass." It is about Christ.

Jesus came as a man to redeem mankind from sin and to show how one is to live in will of the Father. In Matthew 25: 37-40, Jesus talks about how to live:

"Then the King will say to those on his right, 'Come, you who are blessed by my Father; take your inheritance, the kingdom prepared for you since the creation of the world. For I was hungry and you gave me something to eat, I was thirsty and you gave me something to drink, I was a stranger and you invited me in, I needed clothes and you clothed me, I was sick and you looked after me, I was in prison and you came to visit me.'

Then the righteous will answer him, 'Lord, when did we see you hungry and feed you, or thirsty and give you something to drink? When did we see you a stranger and invite you in or needing clothes and clothe you? When did we see you sick or in prison and go to visit you?'

The King will reply, 'I tell you the truth, whatever you did for one of the least of these brothers of mine, you did for me.'"

Take opportunity this Christmas season to share the blessings of Christ with the "least of these."

Take action!

I read this _ _ _ _ _ _ _ times this week.

Positive Influence

What type of influence are you? Life Leaders do things with a
consciousness that others may be watching. No one is an island;
what we do influences others as well as others influence us. The
average person makes decisions only from his or her own
perspective: "What is best for me?" You see that attitude in the
way people drive, especially when they run a red light. Their
only concern is for themselves, not for any other driver. (How
about Christmas shopping in a crowded store?)

Life Leaders have a consciousness that includes other people.
Life Leaders live their life with a positive influence. There is an
insurance commercial currently running that shows a person
helping another and how it affects an onlooker. The onlooker
then helps another person in traffic, and that person helps
someone who has fallen. You get the picture; these people are
seeing a positive example, and are then being examples
themselves. The insurance company calls that lifestyle
"responsibility." I call it good character – putting others before
yourself. In your own actions, you need to consider "How will my
actions influence another?" I remember what we were taught in
a parenting class: "More is caught than taught." Your kids will
mimic what they see over what you teach them.

A Life Leader not only teaches good values, he/she lives them.
Be a positive influence today! As a family project, help someone
who is less fortunate. Get your family involved in the process.

Faith

Romans 12: 10 says, *"Be devoted to one another in brotherly love. Honor one another above yourselves."*

Honoring other people can be in how you act – e.g. the things you do that influence other people. Again, this implies that no one is an island and relates to your speech, driving, your organization or lack of it, even your health. If you are devoted to your family, you will live a healthy life for two reasons: 1) you need to be healthy to take care of them, and 2) they will model the lifestyle you lead – poor health or good health.

If you are an owner/manager, are you being a good influence in the way you manage your employees? Are you showing them honor by giving them proper recognition? Are you reprimanding them with dignity, or do you just "chew" them out?

Are you a person who struggles with anger? Brotherly love says, "I treat others like I want to be treated, and I act with a consciousness that others are watching." Do you encourage your spouse in front of your children, or do you say negative things?

This Christmas season honor someone else. Invite a neighbor to Christmas Eve service and then over for dinner. Invite a single person over for lunch or dinner.

I read this _ _ _ _ _ _ _ times this week.

Positive Influence, Part 2 Don't Just Assume

In my family, we have a rule: whoever is the last person to fill up the trash can takes it out. Until this rule was made, everyone thought somebody else would do it. Well, nobody named "somebody else" lives at our house, so we had to make the rule. The rule was really made for a higher purpose. I am trying to teach my kids to be others-focused. I want them to see the trash and think, "Oh, the trash is full; I had better take it out so the next person won't have to do it or make a mess." I want my kids to "Do to others as you would have them do for you." At their young ages, they want other people – as in their mom or me – to take out the trash, so they are learning the Golden Rule by practice.

During the summer I had an interesting experience. There was a woman with two children, a toddler and baby, standing in the rain on the side of the interstate. Their car had broken down and was so close to the traffic lane that the mother had wisely removed the children from the car. They were standing in the tall grass, so I stopped to see how I could help. The woman did not have a cell phone and had been standing there for an hour!! No one had stopped to help. Everyone had just assumed that help was on the way. I loaded her and her kids into my car and got them off the interstate and waited at a gas station until her husband arrived.

The average person just assumes that whatever the need or problem, someone else or the government will do it or fix it. Life Leaders go through life not assuming that someone else will do what needs to be done. Life Leaders "Get 'er done!" Life Leaders see a situation and take action. Life Leaders clean the dishes, make the bed, do the laundry, pick up the trash in the street, speak out against evil, work to right a wrong or even get involved in taking care of an elderly neighbor. A Life Leader sees

176

a need and says to himself/herself, "I will make a difference. I can help that person." When you live your life helping others, others see it and are prompted to follow your example. Be a positive influence.

Who can you and your family help this Christmas season?

Faith

Jesus said in Matthew 7: 12, *"So in everything, do to others what you would have them do to you, for this sums up the Law and the Prophets."*

In summing up the Law and the Prophets, Jesus meant that all the Law and the Prophets were written to teach people to do good to others. The fruit of the Spirit is others-focused: love, joy, peace, patience, kindness, goodness, faithfulness, gentleness and self-control. (Galatians 5: 22)

A Life Leader considers others in every action. And where you are weak in helping your neighbor or have no motivation, ask God, for He gives freely. Ask God to give you the motivation and the awareness to be others-focused.

I read this _ _ _ _ _ _ times this week.

Obligations and Peace

This Christmas season has not been as joyful as hoped. I have done most of my shopping out of obligation or viewed it as a task. My brain tells me that I am supposed to give because I want to, but I have been so busy that shopping and giving have just been tasks.

Today while in church, I realized that my giving was all self-focused, what I *had* to do. Why do we give anyway? A gift is symbolic of a relationship, caring for another. In many traditions, gift-giving is a sign of favor or of re-establishing a broken relationship. Until today, I had totally missed out on that joy of focusing on others, not myself.

Faith

The Christmas story in Luke 2 has the angels appearing to the shepherds, a truly undeserving bunch. Shepherds were the lowest status of society in Biblical times. Their reputation was so bad that they were not allowed to testify in a court case.

The angel announced to the shepherds in Luke 2: 14, *"Glory to God in the highest, and on earth peace to men on whom His favor rest."*

God came to shepherds to announce His gift. God's gift is His son whom He has given, reconciling the relationship between God and man. I am reminded that my gift-giving is to be out of love, not obligation. My gift-giving is to build relationships, not just honor some tradition.

In God's gift we have peace – peace between God and man.

God's son is a gift. Just as we must choose to receive a gift given to us at Christmas time, we must choose to receive Jesus as our Lord and Savior. Just because God gave it, does not mean it is ours. We have to reach out and receive it. Have you received Christ this season?

Merry Christmas!

I read this _ _ _ _ _ _ _ times this week.

About the Author

William F. Hart's (Bill) life is one of continuous improvement starting right out of college when he went to a motivational seminar. He became enthused with the concept of continual learning and started by wearing out the cassette tapes of the Zig Ziglar series called "How to Stay Motivated." From that he became a life long learner and student of what motivates people and what leads to success in a career and in life.

His mentors have been successful Christian entrepreneurs with a local or national reputation. He is a dedicated husband and father and has a passion for serving others whether as a neighbor, through his local church or as a school board member of an inner city Christian school, Cornerstone Schools of Alabama.. His life is rounded out with an enthusiastic pursuit of high adventure sports.

William (Bill) Hart has a BS in Management from Auburn University 1985 and an MBA from University of Alabama Birmingham, 1989. He has 23 years of sales and marketing experience and has participated in multiple entrepreneurial ventures in the IT, nuclear pharmaceutical fields and medical device fields.

Bill Hart has spent the last 15 years providing career counseling and life coaching as a personal ministry. He celebrates 20 years of marriage and has two teenage daughters. He lives in the suburbs of Birmingham, AL and attends Oak Mountain Presbyterian Church.